tea
party

tea party

20 themed tea parties
WITH recipes FOR EVERY OCCASION, FROM fabulous showers TO intimate gatherings

TRACY STERN
WITH CHRISTIE MATHESON

PHOTOGRAPHS BY BEN FINK

Clarkson Potter/Publishers
New York

Library of Congress Cataloging-in-Publication Data

Stern, Tracy (Tracy Gilbert)
    Tea Party : 20 themed tea parties with recipes for every
occasion, from fabulous showers to intimate gatherings /
Tracy Stern with Christie Matheson. — 1st ed.
        p. cm.
    1. Afternoon teas.   2. Cookery.   I. Matheson, Christie.
II. Title.
 TX736.S75   2007
 641.5'36—dc22   2006015270

ISBN 978-0-307-34643-8

Printed in China

Design by Jane Treuhaft

10   9   8   7   6   5   4   3   2   1

First Edition

to my family
**You have inspired me
to follow my heart
with passion. Your love
and belief in me are what
drive me to make my
dreams come true.**

contents

introduction

Simply having a cup of tea is a beautiful ritual. Unlike other beverages, tea requires a little time to prepare; you need to give it a few moments to steep—to let the flavor of the tea infuse the steaming water as the delicate aroma seeps gently into the air around you and the water takes on a beautiful, glowing color. It's a delight for all the senses!

Tea has a long history of being associated with the finer things. For centuries, in many cultures, it was a cherished (and expensive) treat available only to the upper echelon of society, who would savor every sip and serve it in their best cups. These days it's much more affordable, but vestiges of extravagant associations remain. When someone invites you to join her for tea, don't you feel a little more special than you would if she'd asked you to grab a cup of coffee? Having tea with a friend means you want to spend time with her and relish her company; taking the time to make tea when you're alone means you're treating yourself to something that will stimulate your senses and warm you from the inside out; and planning a tea party—whether it's a simple afternoon tea or a more elaborate themed party—means the ritual of preparing tea will be involved with the event, and that you will be serving your guests a beverage steeped in tradition.

Luckily, though making tea requires just a little extra effort, it's not difficult or prohibitively time-consuming. That means it can and should be a wonderful part of everyday life. And when you celebrate with tea, you can make an occasion special, and make anyone feel like an honored guest any time. You don't need to be a master chef or spend hours in the kitchen to prepare for it. A good tea party should be about enjoying the company of your friends and finding something to celebrate whenever you can.

tea traditions

Tea has been a part of cultures all over the world for hundreds—in some cases, thousands—of years.

CHINA: Legend has it that the Chinese emperor Shen Nung was the first to drink a cup of tea, more than five thousand years ago, when dried leaves from a bush fell into water that his servants were boiling at his request. And thus tea's earliest origins may indeed have had regal attachments. Whether or not the tale is true, tea in China has always been a symbol of status, is often used as part of religious rituals, and has long been celebrated for its medicinal properties.

JAPAN: In the ninth century, a Buddhist priest brought tea from China to Japan and introduced it to the emperor, who enjoyed it so much he began importing seeds for tea plants from China and having them grown in his own country. Over the next several centuries, Buddhists began developing a ceremony around the consumption of tea, and eventually the tea ceremony—ritualistic and almost Zen-like— became a calming element of government meetings and negotiations. In the eighteenth century, a new and practical means of producing green tea was developed, and the drink became more readily available to the masses; in the nineteenth century, that process was automated and green tea became even more widely available. Green tea remains one of Japan's beverage staples today.

ENGLAND: There are many theories about when tea first came to Europe, but some believe Portuguese explorers discovered it in Japan in the sixteenth century and brought it home. Then Catherine of Braganza, a Portuguese princess who married England's Charles II, introduced tea to her new home country in the seventeenth century. Tea's popularity exploded in Britain in the nineteenth century, when the British Empire included India, where the climate allows for the growth of tea. The high cost of importation meant that tea was a huge luxury in England, and those who could afford it kept it locked away in a beautiful teapoy, or wooden box. However, as India started to produce more tea, costs came down and tea became more accessible. The general British populace was delighted to have access to this former delicacy, drinking it many times

tea and me

I became fascinated with the ritual of afternoon tea while traveling in Europe as a young girl with my family. It seemed so elegant and beautiful, and I loved the delicate teacups, the dainty sugar bowls, and the sweets that often accompanied tea. Some children collect dolls or model trains—but after being exposed to the wonders of tea, I started collecting teacups. During my junior year abroad in college, I would treat myself to tea in France's fabulous tea salons. I learned more about the rituals and traditions associated with tea, and about the intellectuals and artists who used to come together over tea to talk for hours. And of course I loved the attention to detail, the beautiful china and linens, the careful table settings, the flowers, and the tasty and pretty treats.

After college, using my by then wonder-

throughout the day. The ritual of tea was harbored at Britain's many tearooms, which were extremely popular in the late nineteenth and early twentieth centuries, and where tea was served with scones, jam, and clotted cream.

FRANCE: The French began drinking tea even earlier than the British (France and Holland were among the first European countries to import tea regularly), and though tea is not omnipresent in France as it is in England, the French have a history as some of the most adventurous tea drinkers. In France there are a wide variety of popular teas, and exotic tea blends are in high demand. The concept of tea salons originated in France, where artists and writers would come together with their society patrons to sip tea and eat pastries. Drinking tea became quite chic, and soon grand hotels began offering elegant afternoon teas, too.

INDIA: Tea's history in India is shorter than elsewhere in the world—the tea industry in India developed in the nineteenth century to meet the British demand for tea, so England wouldn't have to rely on trade with China to get its tea. (The first tea in India was planted in the region of Darjeeling, in northern India.)

Today India produces more tea than any other country. Many of the early tea growers in India became wealthy, meaning tea has come to be associated with high society there, as in many parts of the world. In India, offering visitors alcoholic beverages is *not* the custom—guests are served tea. The majority of the tea produced there is black tea, which is often consumed as chai: tea blended with spices and served with milk.

RUSSIA: The Chinese brought tea to Russia in the seventeenth century, when representatives from the Chinese embassy in Moscow brought chests of Chinese tea to Czar Alexis as a gift. Russia soon established a tea trade with China, but the cost of bringing tea such a great distance was high, and tea was at first available only to royalty and the wealthiest members of society. Tea in Russia is traditionally served in a regal-looking samovar, a combination of water heater and teapot, and poured into glasses held in metallic *podstakanniki*, or tea-glass holders.

fully mismatched collection of teacups, saucers, teapots, and china, I opened The Royal Tea Room in Tampa, Florida. I fantasized about artists, society ladies, mothers and daughters, groups of friends, and couples in love coming together to take tea there. In fact, it was at my tearoom that I met my husband.

When I moved to New York City with my husband, I sold The Royal Tea Room, and

began thinking about ways to share my love of tea with people in my new city. I started playing around with blending teas—in my kitchen I had all different kinds of loose teas, spices, and herbs, so I experimented with combinations. I learned that blending teas is more of an art than an exact science, and I had fun with the trial and error process. It occurred to me that to share my passion I could produce a line of exquisite blended teas.

As I developed my teas, I had a character in mind for inspiration for each one. I thought a society hostess might enjoy something slightly sweet, and I know ladies like vanilla. So I crafted a decaffeinated, vanilla-scented black tea. I now call that the Society Hostess, and it's part of my line of teas, SALONTEA. My Artist tea, a beautifully colored Ceylon tea from the Kenilworth Estate in Sri Lanka, is meant to be lovely and inspiring; the Fashionable Dandy (China black tea scented with bergamot) is meant for the stylish guy who enjoys a dash of citrus. My Musician tea is a soothing blend of rooibos tea with hibiscus and rose, the Romantic is a delicate and lovely green tea with jasmine, and the Writer is a stimulating Indian chai tea with cinnamon, cloves, and cardamom.

I encourage my friends to try blending their own teas based upon their favorite flavors and the teas they most enjoy. Learning how kinds of teas taste, like learning about wine, is not a quick process—but like drinking wine, it's a delightful one. Go to a local tea store and pick up the loose ingredients you think you'll like—perhaps some Ceylon tea, lavender buds, crushed edible rose petals, vanilla tea, chamomile buds, green tea, jasmine flowers, ginger powder, cardamom, cloves, rooibos, Earl Grey tea, or white tea. Blend a few dry ingredients, then brew a cup to see how it tastes. Do you like pumpkin pie? Get pumpkin spice from the supermarket and blend it with black tea. Take a scoop of differ-

ent elements, make a little tea, and see if you like it. Have fun! I also encourage people to try cooking with tea. Tea is a fabulous ingredient in everything from savory foods to sweets. You can use it as an herb or spice, to flavor quick bread and pancake mixes, to poach fish, as a rub for meat, in marinades—the options are almost endless, and it always adds unique flavor. You can even use it in cocktails. Cooking and mixing drinks with tea gives you many more ways to reap tea's health benefits.

tea is good for you!

Aside from its ceremony and history, tea is special because it's so good for you. Almost every week, it seems, a new health study is released touting a new benefit of tea. Tea is a potent source of antioxidants, which have been proven to combat a variety of cancers and cellular damage, from the aging of skin cells to the deterioration of brain cells, by neutralizing the free radicals that cause so much damage in our bodies.

There are a variety of other potential health benefits, too. Green tea has been found to contain fluoride, which fights cavities, to kill bacteria in the mouth, which may help fight halitosis, and to protect against the hardening of arteries by interfering with the oxidation of cholesterol. White tea has antibacterial and antiviral properties, and may help prevent premature aging of the skin. Black teas contain complex polyphenols,

tea primer

There are so many kinds of tea in the world, and it's fun to try different types and get to know what you like best. All tea comes from the same kind of plant, the *Camellia sinensis* bush. Tea plants grow in China, India, Sri Lanka, and some places in Africa and South America. The leaves are picked fresh from the bush, then dried and rolled. Most tea bushes produce more than one thousand tea leaves per year—but one pound of processed tea contains more than two thousand leaves! Some kinds of tea are crushed and exposed to the air in a process called oxidation; many teas are roasted to continue the drying process. Once tea is processed, the leaves are separated by size and grouped accordingly so they will brew at a uniform rate. The highest quality tea tends to come from whole leaves (or leaves that were damaged least during the rolling process). The dust of the leaves (or fannings) tends to go into the lowest grade teas. Even though it's all from the same kind of plant, there are thousands of variations of tea. Here are some of the most common types.

ASSAM TEA: This black tea is named for the region in India where it's grown. It has a strong, bold flavor and is popular as a breakfast tea.

BLACK TEA: This is generally considered the most common, basic kind of tea. It starts as green tea leaves and is then dried (or withered) on racks for up to twenty-four hours, then rolled and twisted to break up the cells of the leaf a bit and allow the leaf to release flavor when it's eventually brewed. Then the rolled leaf is exposed to the air to oxidize, or ferment, and that's when the leaves turn black. It's commonly scented with oils, spices, or flowers. Black tea (unless it's been decaffeinated) contains caffeine.

CEYLON: Sri Lanka used to be called Ceylon, the land from where this tea hails. Ceylon is black tea with a hint of a floral aroma.

DARJEELING: With a reddish gold color and a rich aroma, this black tea is a delicacy. It's grown near the Himalayas.

EARL GREY: This black tea is scented with oil of bergamot, a kind of citrus. It's named for a nineteenth-century British prime minister.

ENGLISH BREAKFAST: A blend of black teas, English Breakfast has a strong flavor and tends to taste best with a little milk and sugar.

GREEN TEA: Tea that's steamed and dried but not oxidized, green tea is celebrated for its antioxidant properties and fresh flavor.

HERBAL TEA: These aren't actually teas—they're not made from tea leaves but rather from a combination of dried herbs and flowers. Herbal teas contain no caffeine. Chamomile, lavender, and mint are common flavors of herbal teas.

MASALA CHAI: This is a blend of Indian black tea and spices that might include cinnamon, cardamom, ginger, cloves, black pepper, and star anise. It's often served with milk and honey.

OOLONG TEA: Best described as a cross between green and black teas, oolong tea is dried for only about eight hours before being partially oxidized. These teas from China tend to be mild and somewhat sweet in flavor.

ROOIBOS: This South African drink tastes similar to black tea, but it's not actually tea—it's herbal, the dried leaves and stems of the rooibos bush. It's red in color and tastes a little fruity, and also blends well with dried fruits.

WHITE TEA: White tea comes from the first buds of the tea plant. It's a rare tea with a light, delicate flavor and pale color, and is naturally low in caffeine.

tabletop tidbits

Snazzy centerpieces or table decorations can elevate a meal from ordinary to exciting. The chapters in this book all offer ideas for dressing a table, which is one of my favorite parts of planning a party. Here are a few more fun ideas for you to use anytime:

- Bowls or glass jars of fruit can be quick, easy, and colorful centerpieces. To give them a modern look, use only one kind of fruit in each bowl or jar. A glass jar of lemons on a pink tablecloth is bright and cheery. A bowl of green apples is fresh and springy. A bowl of Bosc pears can look earthy yet elegant. A bowl of limes is a surprising flash of green. A wooden bowl of pomegranates is chic yet rustic.

- Use conch shells as vases for single buds.

- Use martini glasses as vases for orchid buds or votive candles floating in water.

- Make table runners from rows of horizontal and vertical intersecting ribbons—like the construction paper place mats you used to make as a child. Use one, two, or three colors of ribbons to match your color scheme.

- Use food coloring to dye the water in your vase to match the flowers.

- Line the center of your table with flats of wheatgrass to bring the outdoors in.

- Display a group of small fishbowls with a few pretty live fish swimming in them—and then enjoy the fish long after the party ends.

- Fill wide glass vases partway with sand, stick votive candles or tapers into the sand, and adorn with a few starfish or shells.

- Create an outdoorsy fall or winter display by mixing long sticks, logs, and pinecones.

which are loaded with cancer-fighting, cell-saving antioxidants. Both regular and herbal teas have been shown to improve digestion, detoxify cells, and even help with weight loss by boosting metabolism.

And relative to coffee, full-strength black tea is fairly low in caffeine. Black tea contains about 40 milligrams of caffeine per serving (about half of what you'd find in coffee); green tea has about 20 milligrams per serving, white tea has 15 milligrams per serving, decaffeinated tea has about 2 milligrams per serving, and herbal tea doesn't have any caffeine at all.

Because tea is filled with antioxidants and has so many wonderful health and beauty properties, I don't just drink it. I use it as an ingredient in many of the foods that I cook—it adds great flavor. I also launched a line of beauty-promoting teas and tea-based beauty products: soothing lip balm, eye gel, soaps, lotions, foot soaks, and more. Tea is so good for us—I want to use it in as many ways as possible.

throwing a tea party

I've prepared tea for celebrities at events such as Fashion Week, the Sundance Film Festival, the MTV Video Music Awards, and the Tony Awards. It's amazing how big tea has become. It's not just for ladies who lunch anymore, and I'm thankful for that. But my favorite tea parties are the ones I host for friends and family at home. Even the simplest tea party makes guests feel honored—it's something different, and a treat that they will truly savor.

I have always loved to entertain. My mother was a great influence on me in this vein. She would let me invite thirty girls for a sleepover, and make the best pancakes for all of us for breakfast. I learned that parties don't have to be fancy for everyone to enjoy them—and that having a party shouldn't be intimidating. You just have to do it!

For me, entertaining with tea is natural, and the best way to celebrate anything. Tea is a ceremony in and of itself, so adding tea to a party automatically makes a party more special. Any party can be a tea party if you serve tea! You can serve tea throughout a breakfast, brunch, lunch, or afternoon event; make cocktails with tea; or serve tea along with sweets at the end of a dinner party.

What I love most about entertaining is bringing together friends and family, enjoying their company, and having a wonderful time. You don't need to wait for a special occasion—there's always a reason to celebrate. Once you've decided to have people over (no matter what prompts you), you'll need to plan a few things: decide upon a

theme (even if it's just a proper afternoon tea or sweet dessert tea), pick a color scheme, and think about whom to invite. I try to make every party more memorable than the last—not by working harder or spending more money, but by creating unique themes, decor, menus, and party favors that guests will never forget. This book has suggestions for twenty different modern tea parties. Scale them up and down as needed for the number of guests you want to have—most recipes here can easily be halved or multiplied.

INVITATIONS: Once you've chosen a group of fun and interesting friends who you think will enjoy one another's company, it's time to invite them to a tea party! In our society, paper invitations (along with handwritten notes) are becoming a lost art. So if you're planning a party in advance, why not mail thoughtful, beautiful, funny, or quirky invitations? Send invites four weeks before your party, and ask guests to respond at least a week in advance. Invitations should include all basic pertinent information—the date and time of the party, the location, the name of the hostess, and contact information for a response—plus the scoop on the occasion for the party and its theme, the name of the guest of honor if there is one, and notes on attire if applicable. Of course, not all parties are planned weeks ahead. For a spur of the moment gathering, a simple phone call will do as an invitation. I'll often call friends on a

Sunday to invite them for brunch the following weekend or send an e-mail during the week to plan an almost-impromptu dinner for Saturday night.

DECOR: There's no need to invest large sums of money in decorations for a certain party. Look around your house and find items that you can use to create a gorgeous and memorable atmosphere. And keep your eyes open all the time, at home store sales, antique markets, even dollar stores, and anywhere else you might find unique and affordable home accents—napkins, plates, vases, teacups, tablecloths, glasses, pitchers, place cards, dessert bowls, and more—and start collecting pieces that might inspire your next party.

FLOWERS: Flowers have a part in a beautiful party, but the highlight of the show should be gorgeous place settings and thoughtfully presented food. Flowers should be chosen carefully so they don't overpower the smell of the wonderful food you're serving.

In Victorian times, flowers were never placed on the dinner table—that way, there was no battle between the fragrance of flowers and the aroma of food. Instead of flowers, silver epergnes filled with fruit were often used as centerpieces. Use edible flowers in tea sandwiches for splashes of color or scatter edible rose petals on serving trays or around the table. For flower arrangements, I like to incorporate interesting textures and elements—

not just flowers but greens, twigs, fruits, and vegetables. Even a straightforward bunch of roses are elevated to something special when you gather them in a teapot to enhance the tea theme.

PLACE CARDS: While you don't strictly need to use place cards to indicate where at the table your guests should sit, they do lend a special feeling to all parties. Imagine arriving for a casual breakfast gathering and finding your name waiting for you, presented in some clever way (perhaps painted on a holiday ornament, written on a colored egg, inscribed on a luggage tag, decorated on a cookie, or written on a mini pumpkin). At a party where not everyone knows one another, place cards help people feel at home and comfortable that they know where to sit (and they can serve as reminders about names). For cocktail parties where guests won't be seated, you shouldn't have place cards.

PARTY FAVORS: Like place cards, party favors aren't a requirement for a party—but they certainly make guests feel special. It's wonderful to enjoy a party and have a thoughtful memento to take home, such as a picture frame with an instant photo from the party, a bag of loose leaf tea and a diffuser, sweets, or small candles.

MENUS: The menus I suggest for each party are just that—suggestions. You do not need

ideas and inspirations

Inspirations for imaginative tea parties are everywhere—you just have to see them. If there's an object around your house that you love, think about how you could incorporate it into a party's decor. If you find a beautiful treasure—say, some special plates or cocktail glasses, or a set of delicate teacups—at an antiques shop or boutique, don't think, "I have nothing to use these for . . ." but think instead, "I can't wait to use these for something!" And then use them at your very next gathering.

If you see a lovely place setting in a magazine or catalog, tear out the page and try to re-create it. If you get a zany idea for a fun way to present a new kind of food, write it down. Keep a binder for your magazine clippings, fabric swatches, invitation samples, and anything else that might spark a great idea. And definitely keep a journal that chronicles your parties so you can remember what worked, what didn't, and what party elements you've already used with which guests.

Here are some fun new ideas and old favorites that inspire me and always get tons of compliments:

- **Beets cut into heart shapes:** Ordinary canned sliced beets can transform an everyday salad or a little cracker with a bit of goat cheese into something beautiful and romantic.

- **Lollipops as stirrers for drinks:** What could be more playful and festive?

- **Madeleines as shells for pretty little ice cream sandwiches:** Use two madeleines and sandwich them around a little scoop of ice cream. Press them together to secure, then dip them in colored sugar to make them even more eye-catching.

- **Plain white or colored napkins stamped with your initials,** or the initials of each guest: Use stamps cut from a potato and fabric paint that can withstand washing. They'll double as place cards!

- **Fun ice cubes:** Freeze water into shapes (hearts, circles, letters) using specialty ice cube trays found at home stores. Or freeze lavender, lemon slices, mint leaves, or fresh berries into ice cubes.

- **Lemon rind molds:** Empty the pulp and juice from lemon halves, save the juice for another use, freeze the rinds and use them as little dishes in which to serve sorbet.

- **Coconut snowballs:** Freeze scoops of vanilla ice cream and frozen yogurt in advance of your party. Roll them in toasted shredded coconut for a fast and fun dessert. To up the elegance factor, drizzle heated apricot preserves or chocolate syrup on the plate before serving.

to follow them to the letter. I hope they inspire you to create a menu that works for your event. When you host guests, you shouldn't spend all your time in the kitchen. And you shouldn't need to spend a whole week getting the food ready for a party—if it's that hard, you won't want to do it as often. You can plan menus that are easy and quick but still beautiful and elegant, and the menus in this book should help you do just that. I've included my favorite tried and true recipes in this book—and you'll notice that I

tea sandwiches

Tea sandwiches are lovely little two- to three-bite treats that go perfectly with tea. There are many recipes for tea sandwiches in this book, from basic cucumber to more daring roast beef with pear chutney. If you have a favorite sandwich combination, try it in miniature. Tea sandwiches can generally be made a few hours in advance and stored in the refrigerator, wrapped in plastic, until you're ready to serve them. Whatever kind of sandwich you're serving, here are a few quick ways to add a dash of panache:

- Cut them into pretty shapes with cookie cutters. Think hearts, flowers, circles, and diamonds.

- With the top slices, cut shapes within shapes (for example, a heart-shape cutout in the center of a flower shape) so some of the filling shows through.

- Stack them up. If one layer tastes delicious, add another one or two layers of filling and bread for a tea sandwich with serious height.

- Spread a tiny bit of mayonnaise or butter along the edge of a tea sandwich, then dip the edge into a plate of chopped dill, chives, lavender, or other dried herbs or mild spices. The herbs adhere to the bread and give it a dash of color.

often use prepared ingredients, such as store-bought dressing, chutney, or ice cream. Recipes for the menu items in white type are included in the chapter. It's absolutely fine to serve store-bought foods at parties—entertaining shouldn't be a chore, and if buying food saves you time and effort and makes entertaining easier, you should definitely do it. One of the parties in this book, the Easy Sweet Tea (page 113) calls for all store-bought food—no cooking at all! Just remember to take the store-bought foods out of their packaging and present them in a pretty way.

THE HOSTESS: When you have the privilege of hosting guests for a tea party, take that honor to heart. Even though the parties in this book are easy to put together (and I encourage you to have *more* parties, whatever the occasion), throwing a party requires some thought and effort. Reflect that in the way you put yourself together—why not dress and look the part, whatever the theme of your soiree? Have fun with it, and get into the party spirit. Once you're dressed and feeling fabulous, it's time to focus the attention on your guests. Be gracious, and always be conscious of doing things to put your guests at ease and make them as comfortable as possible. Introduce people, make them feel welcome, and ensure that they have plenty to eat and drink.

brewing tea

To make the perfect pot of tea, you need both a teakettle or a lidded saucepan to heat the water and a teapot for brewing and serving.

- Tea is approximately 98 percent water, so be sure to start with great-tasting cold water. If your tap water has any strange flavor or odor, use bottled or distilled water instead. Don't reheat water that has already been boiled once, because boiling lowers the oxygen content in water and may give you flat-tasting tea.

- For black, oolong, and herbal teas, you'll want to use water at a full rolling boil. For green and white teas, you shouldn't use boiling water—either take the kettle off when bubbles have just started to come up from the bottom of the pot, or bring water

petits fours

Authentic petits fours are bite-size little square cakes that have been covered with fondant or marzipan and beautifully decorated with icing. They are typically made from chocolate or vanilla cake, and they are a very pretty addition to a proper afternoon tea. You can find them at many bakeries and French pastry shops. Nowadays the term *petit four* is used to refer to any kind of bite-size sweet. So if there's something miniature and tasty that you'd like to serve as a sweet ending at your tea party, go for it.

- Pour the hot water into the teapot and let it steep for three to five minutes, according to taste.
- I don't make tea for tea parties from teabags because they aren't very elegant and they tend to contain the dust (or fannings) from the tea-producing process instead of the full or broken leaves, which means the flavor won't be as good. But if you are making a cup from a teabag, follow the directions for boiling water depending on what kind of tea it is. Pour the water over the teabag in your mug, cover it with a lid (or use a saucer), and let it steep for three to five minutes, according to taste.

to a boil, then remove it from the heat and let it cool for a minute or two.

- To warm the teapot, pour a bit of boiling water into it, swirl the water around, and then discard most of it.
- Now add one teaspoon of loose tea for the pot and one teaspoon per person (or per cup of water). You can add the tea directly to the pot and then strain later as you pour, or place the tea in a tea ball or tea diffuser, available at home stores and tea shops, and pour the hot water over it. The first method allows the tea leaves to circulate throughout the water and expand thoroughly, rendering excellent flavor; the second method allows you to remove the tea as soon as it's done to your liking.

For iced tea, let the tea cool, add ice, and then sweeten to taste. Although it is easier to dissolve sugar crystals in hot tea, not everyone will want sweet tea, so don't sweeten it before it cools. To sweeten iced tea, see page 89.

tea etiquette

Having tea is special, even in the most casual of circumstances. And that's a good thing! It makes even the simplest occasion more memorable. Don't worry too much about doing everything exactly right—you should be concentrating on enjoying your guests. But in case you're wondering, here are the most important aspects of the etiquette of tea.

Pouring tea is an honor that should be taken on by the hostess or granted to a guest. Remember, in centuries past, tea was such a prized possession that it would be locked away and cherished as much as anything in the house. While it's no longer quite so valuable, it's still worth treating with respect.

If you're pouring tea, always serve the guest of honor first and yourself last. Pour from the right side of the guest. And always pick up the saucer, not just the teacup.

storing tea

As much as possible, keep your tea away from air, light, heat, and moisture. Store it in an airtight, opaque container in a cool, dry place. Right above the stove where you boil water and the air is moist is not the best place to keep tea! Don't refrigerate or freeze it. Avoid buying tea in large quantities; ideally, you'll drink it within six months of purchase. The longer it's been sitting around, the more stale it is and the less flavor it has.

Don't serve guests cups of tea with teabags dangling from them. To me, that's a bit like offering guests at a dinner party a meal on paper plates with plastic utensils. Beyond being more elegant, tea from loose leaves tends to be of better quality and have better flavor than the leaf dust that goes into teabags. Prepare the tea from loose leaves and serve it from a beautiful teapot. At the very least, keep those tea bags out of sight!

When you're drinking tea, there are a few things to keep in mind:

- The pinky-up gesture that some people associate with proper teas is silly and unnecessarily snooty. Don't do it!
- Drink your tea when it's hot. Unlike during a meal, when you should wait until everyone has been served before beginning, when you're given tea you should enjoy it right away.
- If your tea is too hot to drink when it's poured, place it on the table and let it cool a bit. Resist the temptation to blow on it!
- As you stir your tea, try not to make noise or clink the rim of the cup.
- If your tea is served in a cup with a saucer at a buffet or on a low-lying table, use the saucer—don't leave it behind. Lift the cup with one hand and hold the saucer beneath it in the other.
- When you're done with your tea, if you don't want any more, place your spoon in your cup. If you'd like more, leave your spoon on the right side of your saucer.

NEW YEAR'S DAY
brunch
FOR 8

Start a beautiful, sparkling new year with this **refreshing, invigorating** brunch to help your friends and family relax (and possibly detox) after a late night. It's also a great way to set or keep a new year's resolution to entertain all year. Create an **atmosphere of renewal** with lots of clean-slate white, turn-over-a-new-leaf green, and shiny silver accents.

invitations

Invite friends to begin a new year that sparkles. Use lime green card stock with white text (engraved, thermographed, or simply handwritten in white ink). Send the invitation in a crisp white envelope into which you sprinkle just a hint of silver glitter.

decor

To create a fresh, clean look for this party, start with a background of white and green and then add touches of silver.

- **Fill clear glass vases** with a mix of white flowers and bright green hypericum berries. Coil wide green rubber plant leaves (from the florist) inside the vases if you'd like. For a more over-the-top look, spray-paint tree branches silver and add them to the vases.
- **Line tables** with white or lime green runners, tablecloths, or place mats and sprinkle them with rock crystals or lay crystal garlands, which you can find at many craft stores and shops that carry holiday decorations, between the place settings.
- **Use all white or glass** plates and teacups, inserting a few lime green pieces if you have them, and white napkins.
- **For place cards,** simply write each guest's name in silver on a white place card.
- **Arrange white or glass bowls** of green grapes on the table.
- **For a truly wonderful treat,** hire a massage therapist to give guests detoxifying massages.

music

Play fun, cheerful music with a New York theme—the ball dropping in New York's Times Square is emblematic of a new year's celebration—such as compilations by Bobby Short or Mel Tormé.

party favors

Give guests bags of loose green tea (such as a cleansing ginger green tea) to take home. Tie each cellophane bag of tea with green and white ribbons, and attach a copy of the guest's health horoscope for the year (you can find this online).

menu

Continue the color theme with a delicious—and mostly healthful—menu of green and white foods. Feel free to add other favorites to this list, such as sliced cucumbers with sea salt or watercress tea sandwiches.

green tea

sparkling water with lime

sparkling white grape juice

assorted breads and crackers with goat and feta cheeses,
green grapes, and sliced kiwi

bibb lettuce, avocado, and green apple salad

steamed white and green asparagus with
herbed goat cheese sauce

mini spinach quiches

vanilla tea–infused sponge cake

pistachio ice cream

bibb lettuce, avocado, and green apple salad

SERVES 8

This satisfying salad is also light and healthful, with extra nutrients coming from the green apple and avocado. A sesame–green tea vinaigrette adds a subtle burst of flavor, and more antioxidants. Assemble this easy salad just before serving.

2 heads Bibb lettuce, leaves separated
2 avocados, peeled, pitted, and diced
2 green apples, peeled, cored, and chopped
Sesame–Green Tea Vinaigrette (recipe follows)

Arrange a bed of lettuce on each of 8 plates. Layer the avocados and apples on top and drizzle with the vinaigrette.

sesame–green tea vinaigrette

MAKES ABOUT ½ CUP

This simple and delicious Asian-flavored dressing can be made in advance and stored in the refrigerator for up to a week.

2 teaspoons lime juice
2 teaspoons sesame oil
2 teaspoons sesame seeds
A few drops of soy sauce
½ teaspoon grated fresh ginger
½ teaspoon chopped green tea leaves
⅓ cup olive oil

Combine the lime juice, sesame oil, sesame seeds, soy sauce, ginger, and tea leaves in a small bowl. Whisk the oil into the mixture until it's well blended.

TEA PARTY TIP
If you don't have time to make dressing from scratch, purchase a light sesame dressing and add your own green tea leaves.

steamed white and green asparagus with herbed goat cheese sauce

SERVES 8

White and green asparagus spears are fresh and elegant at almost any meal. You can make the sauce a day in advance and store it in the refrigerator (let it come to room temperature and whisk it for a few seconds before serving), but steam the asparagus fairly close to serving time for the best flavor.

2 pounds medium white and green asparagus, tough ends trimmed
1½ cups (12 ounces) soft fresh goat cheese
½ cup milk
2 tablespoons olive oil
2 cups mixed fresh herbs (such as parsley, basil, tarragon, mint,
    chervil, and dill), finely chopped
Salt

Boil an inch or so of water in the bottom of a large steamer pot, then place the asparagus in the top of the steamer. Cover and steam the asparagus until just crisp-tender, 7 to 9 minutes. Remove the asparagus from the steamer and set aside to cool.

Whisk the goat cheese with the milk, and then whisk in the olive oil until it's thoroughly incorporated and the sauce is smooth. Whisk the herbs into the goat cheese mixture and season to taste with salt. Arrange the asparagus on plates and spoon the goat cheese sauce on top.

TEA PARTY TIP

For an interesting centerpiece, present the asparagus standing upright in glass vases, with the sauce in small bowls on the side.

mini spinach quiches

MAKES TWELVE 2½-INCH QUICHES

Mini quiches are a tea party staple because they can be eaten with your hands and finished in just a couple bites. Spinach quiche is definitely a classic, perfect for brunch, lunch, or a light dinner.

TEA PARTY TIP

Make different kinds of quiche by substituting other fillings, such as chopped sautéed mushrooms, ham and cheese, or roasted red peppers, for the spinach.

1 tablespoon butter

1½ cups prewashed fresh baby spinach leaves, torn into small pieces

One 15-ounce package refrigerated piecrust dough

3 large egg yolks

1 large egg

Salt and pepper

1¼ cups heavy cream

Preheat the oven to 400°F.

Coat 12 individual 2½-inch quiche or tart pans or a standard 12-cup muffin tray with cooking spray. If using individual pans, place them on a cookie sheet.

Melt the butter over medium-low heat in a small skillet. Add the spinach and cook until it turns dark green, about 2 minutes. Remove from the heat and set aside.

On a lightly floured surface, roll out the dough to ⅛ inch thick. Cut out twelve 2½-inch circles with a cookie cutter and press them into the prepared pans. Prick the dough with a fork. Press a square of foil onto the dough in each pan. Bake for 8 minutes, then remove the foil and return the pans to the oven for 2 more minutes, until the crust is light golden.

Meanwhile, in a medium bowl, beat together the yolks, egg, salt and pepper to taste, and cream. Add the spinach and distribute it evenly throughout the egg mixture. Divide the filling among the 12 prebaked shells, trying to get an equal amount of spinach in each shell. Return the pans to the oven and bake for 15 minutes, until the filling is firm. Serve warm or at room temperature.

TEA
PARTY
TIP

Tell your
guests that
in Spain, green
grapes are an
important part of
a new year's
celebration. Many
Spaniards eat
twelve grapes at
midnight (one with
each stroke of the
clock) to ensure
good health during
the coming year.

vanilla tea–infused sponge cake

This is a light and delicious dessert with just a hint of tea flavoring. It's superb with pistachio ice cream. You can make this cake a day or two in advance and store it at room temperature, wrapped tightly in plastic.

4 large eggs

1 cup sugar, plus extra for the cake pan

1 teaspoon brewed and chopped vanilla tea leaves
   (excess water squeezed out)

1 cup self-rising flour

Preheat the oven to 350°F.

Separate the egg whites from the egg yolks, putting the yolks in a small saucepan. Set the whites aside and beat the yolks *lightly,* just to break them up. Add the sugar and heat the pan gently, over low heat, stirring until the sugar has dissolved. Don't let the pan get too hot or you'll cook the eggs. Remove the egg yolk mixture from the heat and pour it into a medium bowl. Add the tea leaves and mix well.

Whisk the egg whites with an electric mixer until stiff peaks form.

Sift the flour into the egg yolk mixture and stir well to combine. Beat in about a third of the egg whites and then gently fold in the remaining egg whites.

Grease a 10-inch Bundt pan and sprinkle the pan with sugar. Pour the cake batter into the pan, and bake for 50 minutes to an hour, or until the cake is light golden and a cake tester comes out clean. Cool the cake in the pan on a rack for 15 minutes, then place the rack over the cake and turn the cake upside down to unmold. Cool for at least 10 more minutes or to room temperature before serving.

PROPER afternoon tea

FOR 6 TO 8

This is the kind of **beautiful, elegant affair** we all envision when we think of afternoon tea: pretty teacups and saucers, silver tiered trays, and delicate tea sandwiches, scones, and pastries to nibble. It is certainly proper, but **it should also be fun!** Invite a group of good friends to get a bit dressed up and enjoy this tea with you.

invitations

Send simple, elegant invitations on engraved or embossed cream-colored stationery (or handwrite in black pen on ivory card stock in your prettiest script or calligraphy), with text that gets straight to the point: "Please come for tea at three o'clock . . . " with all the other pertinent information.

decor

You'll want everything to be traditional, beautiful, and feminine—think pastel colors—but that doesn't mean it has to be perfect.

- **Set the table with your very best china**—but don't worry about whether it matches. At my first tearoom, I always served tea on mismatched china. The guests loved comparing china patterns.
- Always use a **starched and ironed tablecloth.**
- **Use white linen napkins** if you have them.
- **If you have silver,** this is the occasion to polish it and use it.
- **If you have a collection of teapots,** show them off by using them as vases for your floral arrangements—I love to make monochromatic bunches of tea roses.
- **Display the tea courses** (tea sandwiches, scones, and pastries) on tiered silver trays. If you don't have tiered trays, try to vary the height of the foods by placing some on platters and others on cake stands.
- Of course you shouldn't have sugar packets at this traditional tea, but even better than granulated sugar for this tea are **sugar cubes,** which you can find at any supermarket. Put them in a bowl with a little spoon or mini tongs for serving.

music

Play a selection of classical music. Vivaldi's *Four Seasons* is always appropriate.

setting the table

Try not to get too caught up in the rules when setting a table. Above all, it should be beautiful to look at and functional. That said, here are a few niceties to keep in mind:

- Avoid setting places so close to one another that guests have no elbow room and dishes can't be passed or served easily.

- Place the silver (or whatever utensils you're using) in the order of use, with those to be used first on the outside—forks to the left; knives, spoons, and shellfish forks to the right—and those to be used later on the inside.

- A bread plate goes above the fork to the left of the place setting, with a butter knife laid across it at a slight diagonal from upper left to lower right, handle side toward the plate.

- Glasses and teacups go above the knives and spoons to the right of the place setting.

- Depending on how much room you have on your table and how many guests are joining you, you might want to consider setting up a separate tea table so your eating table doesn't get too crowded and passing tea doesn't become too chaotic. If you're setting up a separate tea table, cover it with a cloth. Set it with the necessities: a pot of tea, cream pitcher, sugar bowl, and lemon wedges in a small dish. Place cups and saucers (it's okay to stack them in twos or even threes) at the center of the table. Stack tea plates and small napkins behind the teacups and saucers. Arrange teaspoons near the teacups, and forks (if necessary) near the plates.

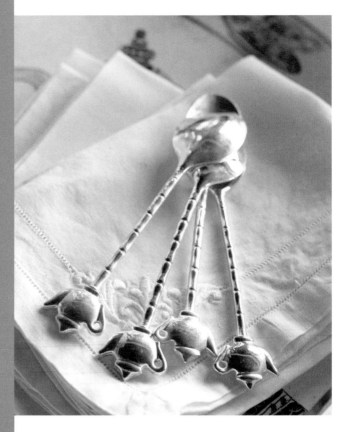

party favors

The menus could be printed (or written in calligraphy) on beautiful ivory card stock that matches the invitations and the place cards and framed for guests to take home. Or **give your guests handmade stationery.** Buy simple, plain card stock and envelopes and a rubber teapot stamp. Use the stamp to decorate each card. Tie sets of cards and envelopes together with a grosgrain ribbon and add a calligraphy pen.

menu

This is a classic three-course tea menu, with scones, savory tea sandwiches, and desserts.

black tea (such as earl grey or english breakfast)

scones with clotted cream
and quince, rose petal, or strawberry jelly

TEA SANDWICHES

cucumber-mint

smoked salmon and chive cream cheese

roast beef and pear chutney

PASTRIES

vanilla tea–infused sponge cake
(page 31; cut into fingers)

black tea brownies
(page 111; cut into hearts)

petits fours
(or other small, one-bite sweets)

scones

MAKES TEN TO TWELVE 3-INCH SCONES

It's great to have a basic scone recipe in your repertoire. Scones are a traditional part of afternoon tea, and I like to serve them at many of my parties, accompanied by Clotted Cream (opposite), flavored butters (page 71), and jewel-colored store-bought jams and jellies.

2 cups all-purpose flour
3 tablespoons plus 2 teaspoons sugar
1 tablespoon baking powder
¼ teaspoon salt
¾ stick (6 tablespoons) unsalted butter, chilled, cut into pieces
1 large egg
½ cup plus 1 tablespoon light cream or half-and-half
Clotted Cream (recipe follows)

This is a basic scone recipe. You can fold in chocolate chips, ground spices, shredded coconut, ground tea leaves, or chopped dried fruit before rolling out the dough if you want something different.

Preheat the oven to 400°F.

Combine the flour, 3 tablespoons of the sugar, the baking powder, and the salt in a medium bowl. Cut in the butter with a pastry blender or a fork.

In a small bowl, whisk together the egg and ½ cup of the cream. Add the egg mixture to the dry mixture and stir until just moistened.

Turn the dough onto a lightly floured surface. Knead until *just* smooth (10 to 12 strokes); then roll out the dough to about a ½-inch thickness and cut out 3-inch circles or other fun shapes (hearts, flowers, animals). Place the cutouts on an ungreased baking sheet. Brush the tops with the remaining 1 tablespoon cream and sprinkle with the remaining 2 teaspoons sugar.

Bake for 12 to 14 minutes, or until golden. Cool on a wire rack for at least 5 minutes. Serve warm if you can, or at room temperature, with clotted cream.

You can make the dough and cut out the scones ahead of time, then store them in the refrigerator for a few days, and bake them just before serving. You can also freeze baked scones for up to a month, wrapped tightly in several layers of plastic. Take them out of the freezer several hours before you plan to serve them and let them come to room temperature. If you want to serve them warm, heat them in a 250°F. oven for 5 minutes.

clotted cream

MAKES 1⅓ CUPS

This is a traditional teatime accompaniment to scones. If you don't want to make your own, you can find clotted cream or Devonshire cream at gourmet markets and specialty stores.

1 cup heavy cream, at room temperature
⅓ cup sour cream, at room temperature
1 tablespoon confectioners' sugar

Whip the heavy cream in a medium bowl until soft peaks form. Whisk in the sour cream and sugar and beat until the mixture is thick. Refrigerate, covered, for at least 4 hours.

cucumber-mint tea sandwiches

MAKES 16 TEA SANDWICHES

This is perhaps the most classic of tea sandwiches, and although it's simple, it's surprisingly delicious. Vary this basic recipe by replacing the mint with dill, thinly sliced radish, watercress, or shredded carrot. Instead of butter, you could spread a thin layer of mayonnaise, cream cheese, or goat cheese.

1 large cucumber, peeled and thinly sliced
Salt and white pepper
16 thin slices white bread
1 stick (½ cup) unsalted butter, softened
16 fresh mint leaves

TEA PARTY TIP

If you want the mint leaf to show through, cut a 1-inch round out of the top circle of bread before placing it on the sandwich.

Sprinkle the cucumber slices with salt and pepper and set aside in a colander for 10 minutes so any excess liquid can drain out. Pat dry with paper towels.

Using a cookie cutter, cut two 2-inch rounds from each slice of white bread. Coat each circle on one side with a very thin layer of butter.

Layer cucumber slices on top of the buttered side of 16 bread rounds. Add a tiny dab of butter and top with a mint leaf. Place another bread round on top, butter side down, and press the sandwiches together gently. Serve immediately or refrigerate, wrapped in plastic, until ready to serve or for up to 3 hours.

TEA PARTY TIP

There are generally three courses at a proper afternoon tea, served on a three-tiered tray. I present scones on the bottom tier and guests start with those, passing clotted cream and sweet jelly to go with them. Tea sandwiches come next and go on the second tier, and the top tier is filled with sweet little pastries. Traditionally, scones are served on the top tier, but I prefer having the sweets on top because they tend to be the most beautiful.

smoked salmon and chive cream cheese tea sandwiches

MAKES 12 TEA SANDWICHES

Smoked salmon on pumpernickel is another quintessential tea sandwich combination. The chive cream cheese adds wonderful flavor and texture.

12 thin slices pumpernickel bread
8 ounces sliced smoked salmon
½ cup cream cheese, softened
2 tablespoons chopped fresh chives

Using a 2-inch round cookie cutter, cut 2 circles from each slice of bread. Using the same cookie cutter, cut 12 circles from the smoked salmon.

Mix the cream cheese and chives in a bowl until soft and creamy. Spread the cream cheese mixture onto half of the bread circles and then top with a piece of salmon and another circle of bread. Press down gently and serve immediately or refrigerate, wrapped in plastic, until ready to serve or for up to 3 hours.

roast beef and pear chutney
tea sandwiches

These are simple sandwiches to make—just three ingredients!—but they have a delicious mix of sweet and savory flavors.

12 thin slices wheat bread
8 ounces sliced roast beef
½ cup store-bought pear chutney

Using a 2-inch wide (or smaller) heart-shaped cookie cutter, cut 2 hearts from each slice of bread. Using the same cookie cutter, cut 12 heart shapes out of the roast beef.

Spread half the bread pieces with a thin layer of pear chutney. Place the roast beef slices on top of the chutney. Add a dab of chutney on top of the roast beef, and top with the remaining bread hearts. Press down gently and serve immediately or refrigerate, wrapped in plastic, until ready to serve or for up to 3 hours.

MOROCCAN
valentine's day dinner
FOR 2 TO 8

This is an **exotic and sexy party**. It's so much more memorable than a traditional Valentine's Day event. When you're planning, think about shades of deep red and gold, Moroccan-style fabrics, roses and rose petals, and **candles everywhere**. The food should be delicious and sensual, not formal or fussy. This party shouldn't be too big—Valentine's Day is an intimate occasion, after all. Invite a few other couples or your best friends, or make it a very romantic evening for two. If you want to go over the top, hire a belly dancer to mesmerize your guests.

invitations

Invite guests to celebrate love with an invitation that looks and smells intoxicating. Use deep red card stock and write in sexy script with a gold pen. Send the invitation in a see-through vellum envelope that—like beautiful lingerie—gives a peek of what's to come. Add a sprinkling of fragrant crushed rose petals before you seal the envelope, and be sure to mail it with a "Love" stamp.

decor

Use the table as a springboard for decorating the rest of the room. Red, gold, Moroccan patterns and fabrics, and roses will make this party gorgeous.

- **Center the meal around a low table** (such as your coffee table). Cover the table with Morrocan-style fabric, which you should be able to find at your local fabric store. Look for fabric with rich red tones. Add an overlay with a golden sheen, if possible.
- **Place large, comfortable floor pillows** around the table and encourage guests to sit and lounge. These can be your sofa cushions or even regular pillows in red pillowcases.
- **If you want to make place cards** even though the seating is so informal, get plain gold tiles (available at tile stores and many hardware stores) and write your guests' initials on them with glass-

paint pens, which you can find at many craft stores. Or buy plain orange juice–size glasses and paint initials on them with a gold glass-paint pen. Pour Rose-Scented Water (page 49) into them for your guests to drink.

- **Keep the lights very low,** and have votive candles everywhere.
- **Think roses!** Have small bouquets of red roses around the room (in glass vases with cranberries in the water), float roses in bowls of water for a centerpiece, and scatter rose petals on the table.

music

Pick up a few CDs of Moroccan music, such as compilations like *Moroccan Spirit* and *Under the Moroccan Sky,* and try to find a range of slower beats and faster, hypnotic rhythms.

party favors

Give guests loose leaf Moroccan mint tea to take home. You can buy it in bulk from a tea shop, then divide it into little cellophane bags. Tie each bag with red ribbon and affix a tea diffuser and directions for brewing, written in gold pen on a small red card. Punch a tiny hole in the card and tie it to one of the ends of the ribbon. If you've decorated glasses with your guests' initials, have them take those home, too.

menu

This menu features several rose-scented treats and dishes flavored with aromatic jasmine tea. Everything is delicious but light enough that it won't interfere with thoughts of romance. If you don't want time in the kitchen to distract you from the party, get takeout from a Moroccan restaurant—order skewers of meat and vegetables to share and couscous, plus a light, sweet dessert.

rose-scented water

rose petal martinis

champagne with pomegranate seeds

moroccan carrot salad

scallop and mango skewers with jasmine tea

jasmine tea–scented couscous

moroccan mint tea

strawberry-rose meringues

rose-scented water

Let guests drink water enhanced with the scent of roses. For eight servings, combine 8 cups of cold water with 1½ teaspoons bottled rose water, which is available at many gourmet food stores.

rose petal martini

MAKES 1 COCKTAIL

Garnish this pretty cocktail with edible, pesticide-free rose petals. Most florist roses are *not* edible, so look for them at a gourmet market or a garden center with an organic plants department. For a sweeter touch, garnish with candied rose petals, which are available in many gourmet shops.

Ice
¼ cup (2 ounces) vodka
2 drops rose water
Dash of lemon juice
Pinch of sugar
2 to 3 organic rose petals, for garnish

Fill a cocktail shaker halfway with ice. Add the vodka, rose water, lemon juice, and sugar. Shake vigorously and strain into a martini glass. Garnish with rose petals and serve immediately.

champagne with pomegranate seeds

Buy champagne that you really like for special events and champagne toasts. This may even be the time to splurge a little! Assume you can serve four guests from one bottle of champagne.

To extract the seeds from a pomegranate, cut the fruit into quarters with a sharp knife. Use your fingers to open the membranes that surround the seeds and collect the seeds in a bowl. Use them immediately or refrigerate them for a few days. Remember that pomegranate juice stains, so wear an apron while you're doing this!

Assume you'll need the seeds of one pomegranate for every bottle of champagne.

Place the pomegranate seeds in a glass or crystal serving bowl next to the champagne. Spoon 1 teaspoon of seeds into each champagne flute and add champagne. The seeds tend to float amid the champagne bubbles, so they look beautiful *and* taste delicious.

moroccan carrot salad

SERVES 8

This light shredded carrot salad is filled with exotic flavors. Make this at least two hours in advance (or up to two days ahead; refrigerate it until serving) so the flavors have time to come together.

> **1½ pounds carrots, peeled and coarsely shredded (about 6 cups)**
> **⅓ cup olive oil**
> **¼ cup lemon juice**
> **⅓ cup chopped fresh cilantro**
> **3 garlic cloves, minced**
> **1 teaspoon paprika**
> **1 teaspoon ground cumin**
> **½ teaspoon cayenne pepper**
> **¼ teaspoon ground cinnamon**
> **Pinch of salt**

Mix together the carrots, olive oil, lemon juice, cilantro, garlic, paprika, cumin, cayenne, cinnamon, and salt in a large bowl. Cover and refrigerate for at least 2 hours. Serve at room temperature or chilled.

scallop and mango skewers with jasmine tea

SERVES 8

This simple, sexy recipe is perfect for a Valentine's Day meal. Scallops are festive and mango is a bit exotic, sweet, and delicious. This would also work with other fruits, such as pineapple chunks or lychees. Be creative! The tea adds a subtle, slightly floral flavor. If using wooden skewers, be sure to soak them in water for ten to fifteen minutes before skewering the scallops so the skewers won't burn on the grill.

> **½ stick (4 tablespoons) unsalted butter**
> **¼ cup chopped jasmine tea leaves**

32 sea scallops (about 2 pounds)

8 skewers

2 mangoes, peeled and cut into large chunks, or one 12-ounce bag frozen chopped mango, defrosted

Salt and white pepper

Preheat a grill to medium-high or a grill pan over medium-high heat.

Melt the butter with the tea leaves in a small saucepan over low heat. Dip a scallop into the butter mixture and then pierce it through the center with a skewer. Add 1 piece of mango to the skewer then repeat until you have 4 scallops and 4 pieces of fruit on the skewer. Repeat with the remaining scallops, butter, mango, and skewers. Season with salt and pepper.

Grill the skewers for about 8 minutes, turning to cook all sides and brushing with extra butter mixture until the scallops are just cooked through. Serve immediately.

jasmine tea–scented couscous

SERVES 8

Think of couscous as a marriage between pasta and rice. How romantic! This side dish features the understated flowery flavor of jasmine tea. It goes perfectly with the scallop and mango skewers, and it couldn't be easier.

1 teaspoon salt, or more to taste

1 tablespoon unsalted butter, or more to taste

2 cups dry couscous

1 tablespoon chopped jasmine tea leaves

In a saucepan, bring 2 cups water, the salt, and butter to a boil. Stir in the couscous, remove from the heat, and cover. Let stand for 4 to 5 minutes.

Sprinkle the tea leaves over the couscous and then fluff with a fork. Season with additional salt and a dab more butter, if desired. Serve hot.

strawberry-rose meringues

MAKES ABOUT 24 MERINGUES

Light, crisp, sweet meringues require just two ingredients—egg whites and sugar—and can be made in advance and stored in an airtight tin at room temperature for a few days. Garnished with strawberries and whipped cream flavored with rose water, they make a nice finish to the meal. Assemble the meringues no more than two hours before serving.

FOR THE MERINGUES
3 large egg whites
¾ cup sugar

FOR THE TOPPING
⅔ cup heavy cream
About 1 pint medium fresh strawberries, hulled
2 teaspoons confectioners' sugar
2 teaspoons rose water

You can make this dessert from purchased meringues and purchased whipped cream. You will need about 1 cup of whipped cream.

Preheat the oven to 250°F.

With an electric mixer, beat the egg whites until soft peaks form. Beat in the sugar gradually until stiff peaks form and the mixture looks glossy.

Line 2 cookie sheets with parchment paper.

Spoon the mixture into a pastry bag fitted with a large star or round tip and pipe 2-inch strips onto the prepared cookie sheets. Bake for about 1 hour, until the meringues are dry and ever so slightly browned. Cool them on wire racks.

While the meringues are baking, prepare the topping: With an electric mixer, whip the cream until stiff peaks form. In a blender or food processor, puree 4 of the strawberries with the confectioners' sugar and rose water and stir into the whipped cream. Slice the remaining strawberries; you will need 24 slices, one for each little meringue.

To assemble, top each meringue with a dollop of strawberry-rose whipped cream and garnish in the center with a strawberry slice.

MAD HATTER'S
tea party

Remember Alice in Wonderland? This **zany, colorful** party—a very happy luncheon or afternoon treat—will put anyone in a good mood, and make guests of all ages **feel like kids**. It's a wonderful tea to throw for a birthday or an "unbirthday" (which everyone celebrates 364 days a year) and anytime someone needs a little cheering up.

invitations

Tell your guests not to be late for this very important date! Cut circles from bright green card stock (or buy circle-shaped green cards from a paper store) and glue on bright pink clock hands pointing to the time the party starts. Write or print all the party details on the back.

decor

Bright colors are the way to go. Come up with a basic combination to carry through as your theme—I'd go with green and pink—but don't be afraid of having things mismatched and topsy-turvy.

- **Start by layering brightly colored table-cloths** on your main table and any side tables.
- **Have a long flat of wheatgrass** as a centerpiece. You can find it at your local florist or garden store; it should be inexpensive and it lasts for a while. Create place cards by writing guests' names on playing cards and sticking them at jaunty angles in the wheatgrass.
- **Bring the outdoors** in with kooky garden accessories like gnomes and rabbit statues.
- **Set the table with mismatched plates and teacups** in cheerful colors. Or use two glass plates at each place, layered with a playing card or a color image of Alice between them.
- **Use mismatched napkins** in a variety of hues.
- Last but not least, **encourage guests to wear hats of all kinds.** Give a prize, such as a bright bouquet of flowers—which you should have scattered about the room—for the best one.

music

The soundtrack from Walt Disney's *Fantasia* sets the right mood for this party.

party favors

Any wacky, colorful gifts will do. Give guests miniature dollhouse clocks to take home. Get small pots of wheatgrass and stick a rainbow of lollipops into them. Give everyone their own looking glasses—vintage-looking hand mirrors. Or offer everyone a copy of *Alice's Adventures in Wonderland* by Lewis Carroll.

TEA PARTY TIP

Many cake designers are making brightly colored "topsy-turvy" cakes, with tiers at wacky angles instead of straight up and down, these days. Order one in advance for a delicious dessert and an eye-catching addition to your party decor.

menu

This menu is filled with fun and fanciful foods that will make the young and young at heart very happy.

earl grey tea

pink lemonade with kiwi

TEA SANDWICHES

ham and banana

blue cheese, walnut, and pear

cream cheese, rooibos tea, and edible flowers

heart-shaped scones with apple butter
and clotted cream
(pages 38 and 39)

eat me! cupcakes

cherry tarts
(See recipe for Mini Lemon Tarts, page 175.
Replace the lemon curd with cherry pie filling.)

vanilla tea–infused sugar cookies
(page 150; cut the dough into hearts, clubs,
diamonds, and spades!)

pink lemonade with kiwi

Purchase pink lemonade, make it from frozen concentrate, or prepare this simple recipe, which gets its pink hue from cranberry juice. This makes enough for a nice big jug or a few medium pitchers.

8 cups water
2 cups lemon juice
1 cup cranberry juice
2 cups sugar
Ice
Kiwi slices or lime wedges

Mix together the water, lemon juice, cranberry juice, and sugar in a large container. Stir thoroughly until all the sugar is dissolved. Serve over ice, garnished with a kiwi slice or wedge of lime.

ham and banana tea sandwiches

MAKES 12 TEA SANDWICHES

Ham and banana might sound like a surprising combination, but they are delicious together. For even more banana kick, make these sandwiches on thinly sliced home-made banana bread.

12 thin slices wheat bread
$\frac{1}{3}$ cup store-bought mango chutney
8 ounces thinly sliced ham or prosciutto
1 banana, cut into at least 12 slices

Using a cookie cutter, cut two $1\frac{1}{2}$-inch rounds from each slice of bread. Spread a very thin layer of chutney on 12 of the rounds. Top those rounds with a thin slice of ham (either cut into a round with the same cutter, or folded to fit on the bread), then add a banana slice and top with the remaining bread rounds. Press the sandwiches together gently and serve immediately.

blue cheese, walnut, and pear tea sandwiches

MAKES 12 TEA SANDWICHES

This is a contemporary tea sandwich with plenty of flavor and a little crunch from the toasted walnuts. The sweetness of the pear balances the sharpness of the cheese.

½ stick (4 tablespoons) unsalted butter, softened
6 thin slices whole-grain bread, crusts trimmed
¼ cup cream cheese, softened
2 tablespoons crumbled blue cheese
½ cup finely chopped walnuts, toasted
½ ripe pear, cored and thinly sliced

Butter one side of each slice of bread.

Combine the cream cheese and blue cheese in a small bowl and mash until soft and well combined. Divide the cheese mixture among 3 of the bread slices and spread to cover the slice. Sprinkle nuts on top of the cheese and then add a layer of pear slices. Top with the remaining bread slices, butter side down, and press down gently. Cut each sandwich into 4 squares or 4 fingers. Serve immediately or refrigerate, wrapped in plastic, until ready to serve or for up to 3 hours.

cream cheese, rooibos tea, and edible flower tea sandwiches

MAKES 12 TEA SANDWICHES

People get a kick out of eating edible flowers, and will love the detail of the presentation. The herbal tea lends a soft, surprising, and tasty flavor to these pretty sandwiches.

1 cup cream cheese, softened

3 tablespoons brewed and chopped rooibos (or other herbal) tea leaves
    (excess water squeezed out)

12 thin slices white bread

20 edible flower petals (such as from roses or nasturtiums), chopped

Mix together the cream cheese and the brewed tea leaves. Set aside.

Using a 2-inch round or flower-shaped cookie cutter, cut 2 pieces out of each slice of bread. Spread a thin layer of the cream cheese mixture on 12 of the bread rounds and sprinkle with the chopped flowers. Cut a small circle out of the middle of the 12 remaining bread rounds and place on top of each sandwich. Press each sandwich together gently and serve immediately or refrigerate, wrapped tightly in plastic, until ready to serve or for up to 3 hours.

eat me! cupcakes

MAKES 16 CUPCAKES

Everyone loves cupcakes—what could be better than having your own little cake all to yourself? You can make these ahead and store them, wrapped tightly in two layers of plastic, for up to two days at room temperature or in the freezer for up to a week.

FOR THE CUPCAKES

16 cupcake wrappers

3 sticks (1½ cups) unsalted butter, softened

2 cups sugar

5 large eggs

2 teaspoons vanilla extract

1 teaspoon almond extract

3 cups all-purpose flour

1 teaspoon baking powder

½ teaspoon baking soda

½ teaspoon salt

½ cup sour cream

1 cup buttermilk

FOR THE FROSTING

1 stick (½ cup) unsalted butter, softened

One 1-pound box (4 cups) confectioners' sugar

½ teaspoon salt

⅓ cup milk

1 teaspoon vanilla extract

1 tube colored decorator icing

Preheat the oven to 325°F. Line 16 muffin-tin cups with cupcake wrappers.

With an electric mixer, beat together the butter and sugar until light and fluffy, 4 to 5 minutes. Turn the mixer to low and add the eggs one at a time, scraping down the bowl between each egg. Add the vanilla and almond extracts and incorporate thoroughly.

TEA PARTY TIP Any cupcakes can be Eat Me! Cupcakes. Make cupcakes from your favorite mix and frost them with your favorite frosting, or purchase plain frosted cupcakes from your favorite bakery. Use decorator icing to spell out the words "Eat Me!" across the tops of the cupcakes.

In a medium bowl, sift together the flour, baking powder, baking soda, and salt. Add the dry ingredients alternating with the sour cream and buttermilk to the butter mixture, and mix until the dry ingredients are just combined.

Fill the cupcake wrappers three-quarters full with batter and bake for about 25 minutes, until the tops are golden brown and a toothpick inserted into the center of a cupcake comes out clean. Let the cupcakes cool in the pan for 10 to 15 minutes, then remove them from the pan and let them cool completely on a rack before frosting.

For the frosting: Using an electric mixer, beat the butter until it's very smooth. Add the confectioners' sugar, salt, milk, and vanilla and mix until everything is smooth and creamy. Frost your cupcakes and then write "Eat Me!" on them in colored decorator icing.

MOTHER'S DAY tea

This beautiful afternoon tea celebrates Mom and all she does. Make it lovely and soothing with a soft lavender color scheme, the **fragrance of lavender** in the air, and springy purple flowers everywhere.

invitations

Craft a memorable invitation from trifold lavender card stock. Guests can open it to find a short, sweet poem or quote about motherhood (such as "A mother is the truest friend we have . . ." —Washington Irving) on the left flap, the invitation information in the center, and a small glassine envelope of dried lavender attached (use glue) to the right flap. Send the invitation in a lavender envelope spritzed with a lavender fragrance.

decor

Create a pretty, relaxing environment in shades of lavender for the guest of honor.

- **Try to get a bunch of flowers** in all different shades of purple and lavender: bunches of lavender, violets, pansies, lilacs, and purple hyacinths (which smell incredible) are all good choices.
- **Fill tall cylindrical glass vases** with purple flower petals floating in water.
- **Cover the table with lavender fabric** or a lavender runner if possible; otherwise use a white cloth.
- If you have any **violet, purple, or lavender plates, teacups, or serving pieces,** use them. Otherwise use dishes in white and pale pastels.

- **Use pale violet or white napkins,** and see if you can find antique-looking brooches (with shades of purple or lavender) to decorate them instead of napkin rings.
- **Write guests' names in lavender ink** on white place cards.

music

Play beautiful classical music such as Bach's Cello Suites or just about anything by Mozart.

party favors

Give each guest a small **lavender-colored photo album,** small bunches of dried lavender tied with a purple ribbon, or lavender soaps, lotions, or candles.

Ask all guests to bring photos of the guest of honor to create a special scrapbook for her to take home.

menu

This is a soothing and delicious menu with lots of lavender and other goodies moms love.

lavender tea

lemon water and lavender water
(see Flavored Waters, opposite)

mini spinach quiches
(page 29)

apple, goat cheese, and lavender tea sandwiches

egg salad with dill on mini corn muffins

scones (page 38; add raisins or currants to the dough, if desired)
with lavender butter

lavender-lemon cake

lavender-honey ice cream

apple, goat cheese, and lavender tea sandwiches

MAKES 8 TEA SANDWICHES

1 apple, peeled, cored, and thinly sliced (at least 16 slices)
1 tablespoon lemon juice
8 slices whole wheat or pumpernickel bread
One 6-ounce log fresh goat cheese, chilled, cut into
    8 thin slices lengthwise
4 teaspoons edible lavender flowers

TEA PARTY TIP For a twist on cucumber sand-wiches, add a few edible lavender buds to Cucumber-Mint Tea Sandwiches (page 40).

Toss the apple slices with the lemon juice to keep them from turning brown.

Trim the crusts from the bread and cut 2 rectangles (approximately 1½ inches by 3 inches) from each slice of bread. Make 8 sandwiches by layering 1 bread rectangle, 1 slice of goat cheese, 2 slices of apple, and a sprinkling of lavender flowers. Trim any excess cheese, and top with another bread rectangle. Press together gently and serve immediately.

egg salad with dill on mini corn muffins

MAKES 16 TEA SANDWICHES

⅓ cup mayonnaise

1 tablespoon Dijon mustard

8 hard-boiled eggs, peeled and chopped

1 stalk celery, chopped

1 tablespoon chopped fresh dill or 1 teaspoon dried

16 mini corn muffins, store-bought or made from a mix

Whisk the mayonnaise and mustard together in a medium bowl. Add the eggs, celery, and dill and stir to blend.

Split the corn muffins horizontally. Divide the egg salad among the bottom halves of the muffins, then top with the upper muffin halves and press together gently. Serve immediately or refrigerate, wrapped in plastic, until ready to serve or for up to 3 hours.

lavender butter

1 stick (½ cup) unsalted butter, softened
1 tablespoon lemon juice
1 tablespoon finely chopped fresh chives
1 teaspoon ground dried lavender flowers
¼ teaspoon salt
¼ teaspoon white pepper

Using a fork, combine the butter, lemon juice, chives, lavender, salt, and pepper in a bowl. Spoon the mixture into two clean glass votive holders or small ramekins and refrigerate for at least 1 hour or up to a day. If you refrigerate it for longer than 1 hour, let it soften at room temperature for 15 minutes before serving.

flavored butters

Make breads and scones even more special by serving them with flavored butters.

- For cinnamon-apple butter, blend 1 stick softened butter with 2 tablespoons store-bought apple butter and ¼ teaspoon ground cinnamon.
- For orange butter, blend 1 stick softened butter with ¼ cup orange marmalade or 2 tablespoons grated orange zest.
- For basil butter, combine 1 stick softened butter with 3 tablespoons finely chopped fresh basil.
- For strawberry butter, combine one 10-ounce package frozen strawberries, thawed, with 1 stick softened butter, ½ cup confectioners' sugar, and 1 teaspoon grated orange zest. Puree in a food processor until smooth.

lavender-lemon cake

MAKES TWO 8-INCH LOAF CAKES

This is a delicious, fragrant cake. You can make it two days in advance and store it, wrapped in two layers of plastic, at room temperature. You can also freeze it for up to one month.

3 cups all-purpose flour
1 tablespoon baking powder
1 teaspoon salt
¾ cup sliced blanched almonds
1½ cups sugar
Finely grated zest of 2 lemons
1 stick (½ cup) unsalted butter, softened
6 large eggs
½ cup lemon juice
½ cup buttermilk
2 tablespoons dried lavender flowers
Lavender-Honey Ice Cream (see box)

Preheat the oven to 350°F. Grease two 8-inch loaf pans.

Sift together the flour, baking powder, and salt. Set aside. In a food processor, grind the almonds with 2 tablespoons of the sugar. Set aside.

Mix the remaining 1 cup 6 tablespoons of sugar and the lemon zest with an electric mixer for a minute or two until fragrant. Add the butter and beat for 2 to 3 minutes, until very light and fluffy. Add the eggs one at a time, beating for 20 seconds after each egg and scraping down the sides of the bowl occasionally. Beat in the lemon juice.

Add the flour mixture and buttermilk in 3 to 4 increments, starting and ending with the dry ingredients and beating on low speed until just combined after each addition. Add the almond mixture and the lavender and mix until just combined. Spread the batter in the prepared pans, making sure it's evenly distributed.

Bake the cakes for about 1 hour, until the tops are golden brown and a toothpick inserted into the center of the cakes comes out clean. Remove the cakes from the oven and let them cool in the pans for about 8 minutes before unmolding them and setting them right side up on a rack to cool.

Slice and serve with Lavender-Honey Ice Cream.

lavender-honey ice cream

Blend 1 quart softened vanilla ice cream with 2 tablespoons edible lavender flowers and ½ cup honey. Let it harden for at least half an hour and up to a day in the freezer. Or simply drizzle vanilla ice cream with lavender honey, available at many gourmet shops.

FASHIONABLE
french tea

FOR 6

Throw a luncheon that evokes thoughts of Paris, Coco Chanel, and the Eiffel Tower in a color scheme of striking **black and white (with a touch of pink** if this is just for the ladies). The British don't have a monopoly on tea—there is a long French tea tradition, too. For this tea, everything should have a **French accent,** from the invitations to the decor to the music to the food. And because France is the fashion capital of the world, everything should be extremely fashionable. If you have any fabulous French designer clothing, this is the time to wear it.

invitations

Find black-and-white postcards of Paris and send handwritten invitations on the back. Invite guests to a *soirée chez moi* and be sure to request that they *répondez, s'il vous plaît*. For a more elaborate invite, buy tiny boxes of French chocolate and send them in a box along with a black-on-white invitation, rolled into a scroll and tied with black satin ribbon.

decor

Build a fashionable atmosphere with a palette of timeless black and white.

- **If you have a glass- or marble-topped table** that recalls the tables in a Parisian café, set it with white or black-and-white place mats. Otherwise, start with a white tablecloth and try topping it with a black runner.
- **If you have them,** use white dishes with a black pattern. All-white china will work, too.
- **Look for miniature Eiffel Towers** online or at a gift store with a French section and place them around the table.
- **Decorate the table** with strands of faux pearls from a very inexpensive costume jewelry store or dollar store.
- **Tie white napkins** with black satin ribbons, and attach white or pale pink camellia pins (available at some fabric and craft stores) to the ribbons. (If you like, the pins can double as party favors.)

- **Make place cards** in the style of French street signs, labeling them *"rue de . . ."* and inserting your guests' names.
- **Make a centerpiece** with white flowers, such as lilies, camellias, or peonies. If you want a dash of pink, find peonies or tulips in the perfect pale shade.
- **Dress yourself** in some combination of black and white, of course. Perhaps a black sheath dress and a pearl choker?

music

Play twentieth-century French standards by Edith Piaf, Josephine Baker, and Serge Gainsbourg.

party favors

The options are endless for parting gifts with French flair. The white camellia pins from the napkins would work, or you could look for inexpensive triple- or quadruple-strand pearl bracelets, samples of Chanel No. 5 perfume, or little French phrase books.

menu

This menu features a variety of French favorites for a leisurely lunch. If you have a signature French dish, this is the perfect time to make it.

darjeeling tea

champagne

vichyssoise

grilled tuna niçoise salad

lavender tea–scented crème brûlée

tea-scented chocolate truffles

vichyssoise

SERVES 6

This is a traditional, creamy French potato and leek soup that's served cold. Make it the day before your party—or at least three hours in advance—so it has time to chill.

½ **stick (4 tablespoons) unsalted butter**
6 medium leeks, cut into 1-inch pieces
4 cups chicken broth
1½ **pounds potatoes, peeled and diced**
1 teaspoon salt
½ **teaspoon white pepper**
Pinch of ground nutmeg
2 cups heavy cream
½ **cup chopped fresh chives**

Melt the butter in a medium stockpot over medium heat and sauté the leeks for about 3 minutes, until wilted. Add the chicken broth and bring it to a boil. Add the potatoes, reduce the heat, and simmer until the potatoes are tender, about 12 minutes. Season with the salt, pepper, and nutmeg.

Remove the mixture from the heat and let it cool slightly, then puree it in a blender in two batches until very smooth. Chill the soup for at least 3 hours or overnight.

Mix in the heavy cream just before serving. Ladle the soup into small bowls or soup cups and garnish with chopped chives.

grilled tuna niçoise salad

SERVES 6

This classic French combination includes an interesting assortment of flavors. It's satisfying but not too filling.

Salt
12 ounces green beans
1½ pounds small potatoes
2 tablespoons Dijon mustard
3 tablespoons red wine vinegar
½ cup olive oil, plus extra for brushing the tuna
Black pepper
1½ pounds tuna steaks, each 1 inch thick
¼ cup drained capers
2 heads Bibb lettuce, leaves separated, washed, and dried
1 pint cherry tomatoes
⅔ cup Niçoise olives
4 hard-boiled eggs, halved
3 tablespoons finely chopped fresh parsley

To prepare the beans, bring a large pot of salted water to a boil. Cook the beans for about 3 minutes, until just crisp-tender, and then scoop them out with a slotted spoon, reserving the pot of boiling water. Cool the beans under cold running water to stop the cooking process; drain well.

Bring the water to a boil again, and cook the potatoes for about 15 minutes, until tender. Drain and then cool the potatoes under cold running water. Drain well.

While the potatoes are cooking, make a vinaigrette. Whisk together the mustard and the vinegar in a small bowl. Slowly whisk in the oil in a thin stream. Season with salt and pepper to taste.

Heat a large nonstick grill pan over high heat or a grill to high.

Brush the tuna with a little olive oil and season with salt and pepper. Grill, uncovered, turning once, until browned on the outside but still pink in the center, 4 to 6 minutes total. Let the tuna stand for 3 minutes, then break it into 3-inch pieces. Transfer the tuna to a large platter and drizzle it with about 2 tablespoons of the vinaigrette. Sprinkle the capers on top.

Toss the potatoes with about 2 tablespoons of the vinaigrette and arrange them on the platter with the tuna. Toss the beans in a bowl with about 1 tablespoon of the vinaigrette and then add them to the platter. Toss the lettuce in a bowl with 3 tablespoons of the vinaigrette, plus a little salt and pepper, and then transfer it to the platter. Toss the tomatoes in the same bowl with about 1 tablespoon of the vinaigrette and add those to the platter, too. Arrange the olives and eggs on the platter and sprinkle everything with parsley. (Alternatively, arrange the salad ingredients on 6 individual plates.)

lavender tea–scented crème brûlée

SERVES 6

Crème brûlée is always a popular dessert and wonderful for parties because the custard has to be made in advance. You'll love having this impressive dish in your repertoire. Try changing the flavor by substituting grated citrus zest or ground spices for the lavender tea.

2⅓ cups heavy cream
⅓ cup half-and-half
1 teaspoon ground lavender tea
½ vanilla bean, split lengthwise
8 large egg yolks
½ cup granulated sugar
3 tablespoons raw sugar crystals, or additional granulated sugar

Preheat the oven to 325°F. Arrange six ¾-cup ramekins or custard cups in a 13 × 9 × 2-inch roasting pan.

Combine the cream, half-and-half, and ground tea in a heavy medium saucepan. Scrape in the seeds from the vanilla bean and add them to the pan along with the bean. Bring the cream mixture to a simmer over medium heat. Cover and set aside for 10 minutes to steep.

Whisk together the egg yolks and the granulated sugar in a medium bowl. Gradually whisk in the warm cream mixture. Discard the vanilla bean.

Divide the custard among the ramekins. Fill the roasting pan with enough warm water to come halfway up the sides of the ramekins. Bake the custards until they're just set in the center, 50 minutes to 1 hour. Remove the custards from the water and refrigerate, uncovered, until cold, about 2 hours. Cover them and keep refrigerated overnight.

Preheat the broiler.

Sprinkle raw sugar crystals over the top of each custard. Place the custards on a small baking sheet and broil until the sugar melts and browns, about 3 minutes. Set the custards aside, uncovered, until the topping hardens, about 10 minutes or up to 1 hour before serving.

tea-scented chocolate truffles

MAKES ABOUT 24 TRUFFLES

What's more decadent—and French—than a chocolate truffle? These little morsels are packed with rich chocolate, and lightly scented with tea. You can make them up to a week in advance and store them in the refrigerator in an airtight container, or freeze them for up to a month. The truffles are best served at room temperature.

⅔ cup heavy cream
2 tablespoons unsalted butter, cut into 4 pieces and softened
2 teaspoons black tea leaves, such as Earl Grey
6 ounces bittersweet chocolate, chopped
1 cup unsweetened cocoa powder

Combine the cream and butter in a small saucepan and bring to a boil. Stir in the tea leaves. Remove from the heat and let steep for 3 to 5 minutes.

Put the chocolate in a bowl and strain the cream mixture through a sieve over the chocolate; discard the tea leaves. Whisk the chocolate and cream mixture together until smooth. Chill for about 2 hours, until firm.

Dust your hands with a bit of cocoa, then use your hands to roll the chilled chocolate mixture into balls. Use about 1 to 1½ teaspoons of chocolate mixture for each truffle. Drop the truffles into the cocoa, turn them until they're lightly coated, and then place them in an airtight container. Store them in layers separated by wax paper.

GARDEN
tea party
FOR 6 TO 10

This festive party is a wonderful way to celebrate the birthday of a good friend over lunch or afternoon tea. If you can, of course, you should have this outside on a beautiful spring day. Incorporate bright flower colors and greens and as many from-the-garden foods as you can.

invitations

Use orange card stock and bright green envelopes (or the reverse) and enclose a small packet of flower seeds with each invitation. Write in white ink, "Let's plant a party where fun is sure to blossom."

decor

Plants, flowers, and shades of spring are key; simply having this party outside will create most of the atmosphere for you.

- **Create an outdoor tent** by sticking four poles into the ground—or into large potted plants in your garden—around your table. Stretch fabric over the poles and tie the corners with twine or ribbon to attach.
- **Place a brightly colored tablecloth** on the table—yellow, green, or orange are all good choices.
- **Have a small potted plant,** such as a zinnia, kalanchoe, or pansy, in front of each plate.
- **Insert garden markers** with guests' names into each pot for place cards.
- **Make a centerpiece from flower boxes** filled with colorful (inexpensive) flowering plants.
- **Create a butterfly garden** in the tent by hanging ribbons from the fabric (attach it with safety pins) and dangling paper butterflies (available at craft and flower shops) from the ends of the ribbons. Stick a few butterflies on wires into the flower-box centerpiece.

- **Use wicker plates** with paper plate inserts if you can find them, or use an array of mismatched colorful plates.
- **Wrap flatware together** in white paper or cloth napkins and tie with garden twine or ivy.
- **For glasses, use mason jars** outfitted with colorful drinking straws.

music

Play happy, springy music. I like to play early Beatles.

party favors

Have the guests take home the potted plants that served as their place cards.

menu

This menu gives a seasonal twist to the traditional tea offerings.

cucumber water and lemon water
(see Flavored Waters, page 69)

iced rooibos tea (or other herbal tea) with orange slices

TEA SANDWICHES

chicken salad and nectarine

cucumber, goat cheese, and sprout

mini lobster rolls

garden salad

corn on the cob with basil butter

strawberry shortcake

chicken salad and nectarine tea sandwiches

MAKES 12 TEA SANDWICHES

Diced fresh nectarines make this chicken salad fresh and special. You can prepare the chicken salad a couple of hours in advance and keep it refrigerated, but it's best to scoop the salad into the pitas close to serving time so the bread doesn't get soggy.

3 large nectarines
3 cups cooked chicken chunks
1 small red onion, thinly sliced
⅓ cup store-bought poppy-seed dressing
5 cups mixed greens, chopped
½ cup chopped walnuts, toasted
3 large pitas, quartered

Cut the nectarines into a ½-inch dice and place them in a large bowl. Add the chicken chunks and the onion. Toss with about half the dressing, enough to coat. Cover and chill for at least 15 minutes and up to 2 hours.

When you're about ready to serve, add the greens and walnuts to the chicken salad and toss to coat, adding the remaining dressing. When you're about ready to go, spoon the salad into the pita quarters and serve.

TEA PARTY TIPS

A wonderful way to sweeten iced tea is with simple syrup. To prepare it, simply add 1 cup of sugar to 1 cup of water, bring the mixture to a boil, stir, and remove from the heat. Set aside to cool. Add to your tea to taste. You can keep simple syrup covered in the refrigerator for up to 1 month.

If you want to serve a cocktail, you can add a splash of citrus vodka to the iced tea.

cucumber, goat cheese, and sprout tea sandwiches

MAKES 12 TEA SANDWICHES

This is another tasty variation on the classic cucumber tea sandwich.

1 medium cucumber, peeled, if desired, and thinly sliced
Salt and white pepper
12 thin slices seven-grain bread
One 6-ounce log fresh goat cheese or 6 ounces goat cheese spread
½ cup alfalfa sprouts
Fresh dill sprigs, optional

Sprinkle the cucumber slices with salt and pepper and set aside in a colander for 10 minutes so any excess liquid can drain out. Pat dry with paper towels.

Using a 2-inch round cookie cutter, cut 2 circles from each slice of bread. Lay cucumber slices atop 12 of the bread rounds and season with salt and pepper. Sprinkle sprouts on top of the cucumber slices.

Cut the goat cheese log into 12 thin slices and lay a slice of goat cheese atop 12 of the bread rounds. Sprinkle sprouts over the cheese and then top with cucumber slices. Top with the remaining 12 bread rounds. Press the sandwiches together gently and garnish each sandwich with a slice of cucumber and a sprig of dill, if desired. Serve immediately or refrigerate, wrapped in plastic, until ready to serve or for up to 3 hours.

mini lobster rolls

The best lobster salad is very simple: use fresh lobster meat and let it be the star of the show. You can make the salad a few hours in advance—if you do, keep it covered in the refrigerator until you're ready to prepare the sandwiches. This recipe makes plenty of mini rolls, which is good because your guests will want more than one, and probably more than two!

12 ounces cooked shelled lobster meat, cut into ½-inch chunks
½ cup mayonnaise
½ cup finely diced celery
1 tablespoon minced fresh dill
Salt and white pepper
8 hot dog buns

Combine the lobster, mayonnaise, celery, and dill with salt and pepper to taste. Trim the ends from the hot dog buns and then cut each bun in half. Fill the buns and serve.

garden salad

SERVES 8

A "garden" salad can have whatever you like in it. To vary the version here, add diced yellow or red peppers, corn kernels, diced red onion, thinly sliced radishes, or your favorite salad vegetables. Fresh herbs give this a flavor boost; try substituting basil, tarragon, or cilantro for the mint.

    2 tablespoons lemon juice
    1/3 cup olive oil
    Salt and pepper
    8 cups mixed greens
    1 pint grape tomatoes
    2 large avocados, peeled, pitted, and cut into 1-inch chunks
    2 medium carrots, peeled and shredded
    1 medium cucumber, sliced
    1/4 cup thinly sliced fresh mint leaves

In a large bowl, whisk together the lemon juice, olive oil, and salt and pepper to taste. Toss the greens with the dressing to coat. Add the tomatoes, avocados, carrots, cucumber, and mint. Season with salt and pepper and toss again.

corn on the cob with basil butter

SERVES 8

Corn on the cob is delicious with all kinds of flavored butters. See page 71 for more ideas.

1 stick (½ cup) salted butter, softened
2 tablespoons chopped fresh basil
Salt and pepper
8 ears corn, husked

Stir together the butter and the basil, season with salt and pepper, and set aside.

Bring a large pot of water to a boil. Add the corn to the pot, bring the water back to a boil, and cook the corn for 4 minutes.

Drain well and spread the corn with basil butter. Serve hot.

strawberry shortcake

SERVES 6

This simple and delicious recipe is always a crowd-pleaser. You can find buttermilk biscuits at most grocery stores and bakeries, making this an easy no-bake dessert. You can make the whipped cream up to a day in advance and refrigerate it until you're ready to serve, and you'll need to give the strawberries about a half hour to macerate. Assemble just before serving.

2½ pounds strawberries, hulled and quartered (about 8 cups)
½ cup granulated sugar
1 cup heavy cream
¼ cup sour cream
2 tablespoons confectioners' sugar
½ teaspoon vanilla extract
Six 3-inch buttermilk biscuits

Toss the strawberries with the granulated sugar in a large bowl and let them stand for 5 minutes. Mash the strawberries ever so gently with a fork. Let the mashed strawberries stand at room temperature, stirring occasionally, for about 30 minutes.

Meanwhile, with an electric mixer beat together the heavy cream, sour cream, confectioners' sugar, and vanilla on medium-high speed until soft peaks form.

Split the biscuits horizontally and place the halves, split side up, on 6 plates. Top with the strawberries and their juices, and then with the whipped cream.

CHAI breakfast

FOR 6 TO 8

Chai tea has become extremely popular everywhere from teahouses to coffee chains. It's a wonderfully **aromatic** Indian version of tea made from black tea, spices, and milk. Since this is for breakfast (or brunch), there's no need to go over the top with decorations, but play up an **Indian theme** with brightly colored table runners and Indian music.

invitations

Tempt guests to come to this delicious breakfast and "discover a distant place" at your home. Use simple, rough-edged cream or ivory cards adorned with a stamp resembling henna art (available at paper stores and online) in a shade of deep red or rust. Use a pen in the same color to write the invitation details inside the card and to address the matching envelopes.

decor

Keep the decor fairly simple for this breakfast. I like orange and brown, but rich reds or other gloriously deep, saturated colors would also be appropriate.

- **Line the table** with placemats and napkins in orange and brown, or to match your color scheme.
- **Use orange, brown, white, and red dishes** if you have them—otherwise white dishes will work nicely with the brightly colored placemats and napkins.
- **If you can find cards** with an elegant elephant motif, use those for place cards— look for them at a stationery store.
- **Place small bowls** of loose chai tea around the table.

music

Play a variety of Indian music—chants, sitar, current pop, and classical. Anything by Ravi Shankar is a good choice.

party favors

Give guests softly fragrant incense, preferably in sweet spice flavors such as cinnamon and cardamom. Add an incense holder and matches to make a complete set. Or offer a jar of addictive Chai Candied Almonds (page 101) to take home.

menu

This simple menu is delicious for a breakfast, brunch, or anytime you want a little spice.

chai tea with milk and honey

yogurt and granola

fresh fruit

chai candied almonds

chai tea pancakes

chai tea with milk and honey

You can find chai tea and chai tea mixes at most grocery stores and gourmet shops, but if you want to make your own, try this recipe for something truly special.

1 quart water
1 quart whole milk
½ teaspoon ground cardamom
½ teaspoon black pepper
½ teaspoon ground cloves
½ teaspoon ground cinnamon
½ teaspoon ground nutmeg
1 vanilla bean, split lengthwise and scraped, or ½ teaspoon vanilla extract
4 teaspoons chopped black tea leaves
½ cup honey

Combine the water and milk in a large saucepan and bring to a boil. Reduce the heat to very low. Add the cardamom, pepper, cloves, cinnamon, nutmeg, and vanilla bean pod and seeds. Cover and simmer gently for 12 minutes.

Remove from the heat, add the tea, and let steep for 5 minutes. Strain the chai into a pitcher, add the honey, and mix well. Serve hot or cold.

granola

MAKES ABOUT 10 CUPS

This recipe makes more than you'll need for this breakfast, but you'll enjoy the leftovers. Granola is tasty with fruit and yogurt, and also with milk for breakfast or sprinkled over ice cream for dessert. Make this granola up to a week ahead. Store it at room temperature in an airtight container.

4 cups rolled oats
2½ cups chopped pecans
1½ cups sweetened flaked coconut
¼ teaspoon salt

½ cup vegetable oil
½ cup honey
1 cup dried cranberries
1 cup raisins

Preheat the oven to 375°F. Line a large, shallow baking pan with foil and spray the foil with cooking spray.

Toss together the oats, pecans, coconut, and salt in a large bowl. Whisk together the oil and honey and then stir into the oat mixture until well coated. Spread the entire mixture into the prepared baking pan and bake, stirring occasionally, until golden brown, 25 to 30 minutes.

Remove from the oven and stir in the cranberries and raisins. Let the granola cool completely before serving or storing.

chai candied almonds

MAKES 4 CUPS

These are a heavenly and healthy snack. The aroma that fills your kitchen when you make them is better than the fragrance coming from the best nut street vendors in New York City! They are delicious on their own, on top of vanilla ice cream, in salads, and on top of pancakes.

To make a thoughtful gift, place these almonds in a nice glass jar and attach a hand-written note with the recipe.

1 large egg white
4 cups almonds
½ cup sugar
¼ teaspoon salt
½ teaspoon ground cinnamon
½ teaspoon ground chai tea

Preheat the oven to 250°F. Spray a rimmed baking sheet with cooking spray.

Lightly beat the egg white with 1 teaspoon of water in a large bowl until frothy. Add the nuts and stir until they're coated. In a separate bowl, whisk together the sugar, salt, cinnamon, and tea. Toss well with the nuts. Spread the nuts onto the prepared baking sheet and bake for about an hour, stirring occasionally, until the nuts are browned. Remove from the oven and let cool completely.

chai tea pancakes

SERVES 8

You could simply flavor pancakes with cinnamon, but chai tea gives a more complex and special flavor.

2 cups all-purpose flour
3 tablespoons sugar
1 tablespoon baking powder
½ teaspoon salt
2 cups buttermilk
3 large eggs, separated
1½ teaspoons vanilla extract
2 tablespoons ground chai tea
Maple syrup, for serving
Yogurt, for serving (optional)
Granola (page 100), for serving (optional)
Chai Candied Almonds (page 101)

TEA PARTY TIP **Don't want to make pancakes from scratch? Just stir ground chai tea (about ½ teaspoon per serving) into instant pancake mix to add a subtly exotic flavor to a breakfast and brunch staple.**

Whisk together the flour, 2 tablespoons of the sugar, the baking powder, and salt in a large bowl. Add the buttermilk, egg yolks, and vanilla and whisk until smooth. The batter should be nice and thick.

Use an electric mixer to beat the egg whites until soft peaks form. Add the remaining 1 tablespoon sugar to the egg whites and beat until stiff but not dry. Fold the egg whites into the batter and then fold in the ground tea.

Spray a griddle or a large heavy skillet with cooking spray (keeping the spray on hand for when your surface starts to stick). Heat over medium-low heat. Working in batches, pour the batter, about 3 tablespoons at a time, onto your griddle or skillet. Cook until the pancakes are golden brown, 2 to 3 minutes per side. Transfer to warmed plates. Serve, topped with syrup, yogurt and Granola, if using, and Chai Candied Almonds.

GENTLEMEN'S
tea

Tea parties aren't just for the ladies! You can host a tea for your father, brother, husband, boyfriend, or good friend. The setting should be classic, the decor should be reminiscent of an **old-school gentlemen's club** (perhaps with **plaid accents** or images from British hunt scenes), and the food should appeal to a manly but refined palate. This could be a late lunch (complete with martinis and scotch) or an early cocktail party.

invitations

Set a classic tone with handwritten invitations on rough-edged, dark ivory paper. Roll the paper like a scroll, tie it with plaid ribbon, and send it in a small box or tube, which you can find at specialty mailing centers; write the address directly on the tube.

decor

Create a club-like atmosphere—simple and straightforward with nothing frilly or dainty.

- **Host this tea in the most masculine room** in your home—if you have a family room with leather club chairs, a dark wood-paneled dining room, or a study with walls painted burgundy or hunter green, that's the place.
- **Don't get too fussy with table linens.** Use a wooden table lined with a gray flannel or tartan plaid runner and place mats and napkins that match the color scheme.
- **Get out your simplest,** most classic white dinnerware, teacups, and serving pieces and basic silverware.
- **Skip the flowers** and create arrangements with greens and branches or potted ivy.

- **Keep the place cards simple:** ivory card stock with hunter green or burgundy writing.

music

Play powerful classical music—maybe a symphony by Mahler—or lighten things up and play a little jazz.

party favors

Send the men home with one great cigar wrapped in cellophane tied with a plaid ribbon along with a tin of yerba maté or Earl Grey tea.

maté cups

The traditional way to serve yerba maté—an herbal tea that comes from a South American holly shrub—is in a maté cup that resembles the shape of a hollowed-out gourd. You brew the loose tea directly in the cup, and then sip it through a bombilla, a special straw with a filter. Tradition holds that the health benefits derived from yerba maté (it's a stress reliever and reputed to boost metabolism, and it's packed with antioxidants) are more potent when the tea is ingested in this way. Of course, you can also brew and serve it just as you would any other kind of tea.

menu

You can still apply the classic tea combination of sandwiches, scones, and sweets—as long as the elements are hearty and the flavors strong.

black tea martinis (page 120)

yerba maté or earl grey tea

cheese scones

welsh rarebit

apple sausage sandwiches with hot mustard, tomato, and arugula

roast beef and pear chutney tea sandwiches
(page 43)

black tea brownies

scotch

cheese scones

MAKES 12 TO 14 SCONES

Scones go from sweet to savory when they're baked with Cheddar cheese and chives. You can bake these in advance and then keep them wrapped in a few layers of plastic wrap at room temperature for a day or two. Unwrap and heat them for five minutes in a three-hundred-degree oven before serving.

2¾ cups all-purpose flour
1 tablespoon sugar
2 teaspoons baking powder
¾ cup minced fresh chives
1 cup (4 ounces) shredded sharp Cheddar cheese
¾ cup whole milk, chilled, or more if needed
2 large eggs
1 tablespoon vegetable oil
2 teaspoons Dijon mustard
Softened butter, for serving

Preheat the oven to 425°F.

Sprinkle a large baking sheet with flour. Whisk the flour, sugar, and baking powder together in a large bowl. Stir in the chives and cheese and set aside. In a small bowl, whisk together the milk, one of the eggs, the oil, and the mustard. Gradually add the milk mixture to the dry ingredients, mixing (but not overmixing!) until moist clumps form. Add more milk in tablespoon increments if the dough seems too dry. Turn the dough onto a lightly floured surface and knead until the dough just comes together.

Pat the dough into a 1-inch-thick round. Use a 2½-inch round cutter to cut out scones. Gather your dough scraps and repeat the process. Transfer the scones to the prepared baking sheet. Lightly beat the remaining egg in a small dish and brush it over the scones. Bake the scones until they're golden on top and a tester or toothpick inserted into the center comes out clean, about 14 minutes. Cool the scones on the sheet for about 5 minutes. Serve warm with softened butter.

welsh rarebit

SERVES 8

This savory British dish is basically cheese on toast, but it has extra zip from beer and Dijon mustard. The guys at the party will love this treat.

8 slices white bread, toasted

2 cups (8 ounces) shredded sharp Cheddar cheese

5 tablespoons beer

3 tablespoons butter

2 tablespoons Dijon mustard

1 cup soft, fresh white bread crumbs

On a large baking sheet, arrange the toast slices so that their sides are touching. Combine the cheese, beer, butter, and mustard in a medium saucepan. Stir over medium-low heat until the mixture is smooth. Remove from the heat and stir in the bread crumbs. Spoon over the bread slices to cover. (You can do this 3 or 4 hours in advance of your party and chill until you're almost ready to serve.)

Preheat your broiler.

Broil the open-faced sandwiches until the topping starts to brown, about 2 minutes (or slightly longer if they've been refrigerated). Keep a close eye on them to make sure they don't burn, and rotate the baking sheet to encourage even broiling if necessary. Cool for 2 minutes, then cut each piece into halves or quarters, and serve.

apple sausage sandwiches with hot mustard, tomato, and arugula

MAKES 8 SANDWICHES

These are no prim little tea sandwiches—they're hearty and have plenty of kick.

**Eight 6-inch precooked apple sausages (or other fully cooked sausages),
cut in half lengthwise**
1 stick (½ cup) unsalted butter, softened
2 baguettes (about 14 inches by 4 inches), cut in half horizontally
5 tablespoons prepared hot English mustard
2 large tomatoes, thinly sliced
2 large bunches of arugula

Heat the sausages, cut side down, in a large nonstick skillet over medium heat until they're hot throughout and starting to brown, about 4 minutes per side. Remove from the heat.

Spread the butter over the cut sides of the bread. Spread the mustard over the butter. Arrange the tomato slices and arugula on the bottom halves of the bread and then top them with the sausages. Top with the remaining bread. Cut each baguette crosswise into 4 sandwiches and serve immediately, while they're still warm.

black tea brownies

MAKES SIXTEEN 2-INCH BROWNIES

Use the best quality chocolate you can find to make these really sinful. The tea gives them an understated, unexpected flavor that works beautifully with chocolate. Make these a day or two ahead and store them at room temperature in an airtight container between layers of wax paper.

2 sticks (1 cup) unsalted butter
8 ounces bittersweet chocolate, coarsely chopped
1¼ cups all-purpose flour
1 teaspoon baking powder
½ teaspoon salt
2 cups sugar
4 large eggs
2 teaspoons vanilla
¼ cup chopped black tea leaves

Preheat the oven to 350°F. Grease a 9-inch square baking pan, line the bottom and sides with parchment paper, and grease the paper.

Melt the butter and chocolate in a medium heat-proof bowl over a saucepan of simmering water, or in the microwave, stirring occasionally, until smooth.

Whisk together the flour, baking powder, and salt in a small bowl.

Whisk together the sugar, eggs, and vanilla in a large bowl, then pour in the chocolate mixture, and whisk until well combined. Whisk in the flour mixture, then stir in the tea leaves and transfer the batter to the prepared baking pan.

Bake until the top is shiny and set and the sides have just started to pull away from the pan, 35 to 40 minutes.

Cool the brownies completely in the pan on a rack. Invert them onto a cutting board, remove the paper, and cut into squares.

EASY
sweet tea
FOR 4 TO 6

A sweet tea, or all-dessert tea, is very popular at most tea-rooms. What could be better than sharing a selection of cakes and pastries and a pot of tea with a few friends? This is a fun tea to have with a small group of guests in the **afternoon or after dinner,** but of course you could make more tea and have more desserts and invite as many guests as you'd like. You can put this tea together entirely from **store-bought items**—you have no excuses not to throw a tea party when it's this easy!

invitations

Keep invitations simple—**search for vintage postcards of cake or desserts** and send them in bright pink envelopes to invite friends to partake in "sweets for the sweet." You might stamp the flap with an image of something sweet such as a piece of cake—check a paper store or online to find a stamp you like.

decor

Keep the decorations minimal for this sweet little tea, and certainly don't set a formal table—there don't need to be any plates to wash for this one. While I love to serve this tea around a fireplace if I can because it's so cozy, you can really have it anywhere, anytime.

- **Find a large, simple silver tray** to serve as your tea tray and lay a linen napkin on it.
- **Place all the sweet treats** on a pretty cake stand.
- **Load the tray with the plate of sweets,** a teapot, several teacups and saucers, teaspoons, sugar and cream, and little pink or white napkins. There's no need for plates, as all of the sweets should be just a bite or two.
- **If you want flowers,** a bouquet of white or pink tulips or roses (or a mix of both) will do the trick!

music

Play something dreamy, like *Debussy for Daydreaming*—utterly classic— or Madeleine Peyroux's *Dreamland* if you want something less traditional.

party favors

Be sure to give each guest a few of their favorite sweets from the tea, wrapped in a cellophane bag and tied with ribbon, to take home.

menu

This menu is so easy to plan. Stop by your favorite bakery and see what little sweets look especially good; the menu below is just a suggestion. Figure about five to seven small pastries per person. Brew a pot of tea and you're ready!

hearty black tea, such as earl grey

napoleons or mini eclairs

miniature fruit tarts

madeleines, dusted with confectioners' sugar

petits fours

sponge cake, cut into hearts

fresh berries

Please come for a

Spa Night

bridal shower for

Hillary

No need to book an appointment—just be there!

May 12

The pampering begins at 6 p.m.

(*sweats only* 212.552.5673)

BRIDAL SHOWER
(girls' night in)

Go beyond the typical bridal shower activities and create a party the bride-to-be and her friends will really love: a **spa night** that helps everyone relax and have a great time. Serve healthful, delicious foods buffet style, and offer a selection of fun **tea-based martinis**.

invitations

Give guests a hint of what's to come by sending an invitation on white card stock attached with a turquoise ribbon to turquoise card stock (mailed in a vellum envelope) that includes a list of spa services that will be available on the night of the shower: manicures, pedicures, foot soaks, eye masks, or maybe even massages.

decor

Re-create the spa experience at home! From "waiting area" to "treatment areas" to the food setup, make everything beautiful and soothing and clean. When thinking about color, go with clean white and shades of green and turquoise.

- **Set up a waiting area** filled with current women's magazines galore. Be sure there's plenty of comfortable seating.
- **Establish treatment areas** with chairs, fluffy white towels, and spa products, such as hand and foot lotions, foot soaks, masks, and scrubs.
- **Have all guests contribute** in advance and hire a manicurist and a pedicurist and perhaps even a massage therapist—contact a local spa or salon for recommendations—for the night.
- **For guests not getting a treatment** from a pro at any given time, have little plastic foot-soaking tubs filled with warm water and foot soaks or mineral salts (change the water and soak between each use) and rejuvenating eye masks chilling in the fridge.
- **Have turquoise spa flip-flops** (possibly printed with the date) for everyone to put on at the start of the night.
- **Set up different drink and food stations** on tables decorated with bamboo shoots or white orchids, both of which have a Zen-like, tranquil spa feel.
- **Set out turquoise and green cocktail napkins,** martini glasses, white salad plates, forks and spoons, and glass dessert bowls for the frozen yogurt and sorbet bar.

music

Play soothing spa-style instrumentals (*Spa Lounge* and *Sounds of Spa: Serenity* are two good compilations) at the beginning of the night to help everyone relax. If you're planning to go out after the spa night, crank it up toward the end of the evening with dance-ready songs (Madonna is a must).

party favors

Guests can take home their spa flip-flops and turquoise-colored goody bags filled with a few travel-size spa and beauty products from the drugstore or a local spa.

menu

Instead of a seated meal, serve martinis, mineral water, and healthful food, buffet style. Tempt your guests with a colorful array of tea-filled libations. Have chilled martini glasses, ice, and cocktail shakers ready to go. Set up a salad bar with fresh mixed greens, fresh vegetables, fruits, nuts, and dried cranberries, plus an assortment of light vinaigrettes. Follow it with a tempting but healthful dessert bar with three kinds of frozen yogurt and two kinds of sorbet, plus delicious healthy toppings such as fresh fruit and granola and whipped cream.

MARTINI BAR

black tea martinis

green tea martinis

white tea martinis with coconut

cranberry tea cosmopolitans

mineral water with lime

sophisticated salad bar

frozen yogurt and sorbet bar

black tea martini

Make these one at a time, to order, for your guests. Brew and chill the tea in advance.

¼ cup (2 ounces) vodka
¼ cup (2 ounces) brewed black tea, chilled
Ice
Chopped black tea leaves
Sugar

Shake the vodka and tea together in a cocktail shaker with ice. On a shallow plate, mix together enough tea leaves and sugar for the rim of a martini glass. Moisten the rim of a chilled martini glass with water and then dip it into the tea leaves and sugar. Strain the martini mixture into the prepared glass.

green tea martini
Substitute brewed green tea and green tea leaves for the black tea and black tea leaves in the Black Tea Martini.

white tea martini with coconut
Substitute brewed white tea and dried shredded coconut for the black tea and black tea leaves in the Black Tea Martini.

cranberry tea cosmopolitan

MAKES 1 COCKTAIL

This is a tea-infused version of a classic girly cocktail. It almost wouldn't be a bridal shower without it.

> **2 tablespoons (1 ounce) vodka**
> **1 tablespoon (½ ounce) triple sec**
> **1 tablespoon (½ ounce) cranberry juice, chilled**
> **1 tablespoon (½ ounce) cranberry herbal tea, chilled**
> **Splash of lime juice**
> **Ice**
> **Lime wedge, for garnish**

Combine the vodka, triple sec, cranberry juice, cranberry tea, and lime juice in a cocktail shaker with some ice and shake. Strain into a chilled martini glass, garnish with a lime wedge on the rim, and serve.

sophisticated salad bar

SERVES 6 TO 8

Here's a suggested list of what to buy. While you'll probably have some leftovers, you want the salad bar to look amply stocked. Present each element in individual serving bowls with serving utensils, serve the dressings in bowls with spoons or in squeeze bottles, and stack salad plates or bowls and salad forks nearby.

> **12 cups mixed greens**
> **One 16-ounce can sliced beets, drained**
> **2 pints cherry or grape tomatoes**
> **12 ounces sugar snap peas**
> **3 large pears, cored and sliced**
> **Two 11-ounce cans mandarin orange sections, drained**

2 pints strawberries, hulled and sliced

2 cups (8 ounces) goat cheese, crumbled

2 cups (8 ounces) Gorgonzola, crumbled

2 cups pecan or walnut halves

2 cups dried cranberries

An assortment of store-bought light vinaigrettes, such as balsamic
and strawberry

frozen yogurt and sorbet bar

SERVES 6 TO 8

Here's a suggested list of what to have on hand. As with the salad bar, you'll have leftovers, but you want the display to appear well-stocked.

1 quart vanilla frozen yogurt

1 quart chocolate frozen yogurt

1 pint strawberry or raspberry frozen yogurt

1 pint lemon sorbet

1 pint mango or coconut sorbet

2 pints strawberries, hulled and sliced

1 pint raspberries

1½ cups apricot preserves, heated

One 14-ounce can real whipped cream

2 cups Granola (page 100)

2 cups mini M&Ms, chocolate chips, or white chocolate chips

1 cup flaked coconut

1 cup fresh mint leaves

ENGAGEMENT
dinner
FOR 8

Two lovebirds have decided to get married. It's a time to celebrate with a romantic fall dinner with friends—or maybe for the families, who could be meeting for the first time. This should be **warm, beautiful, intimate,** and both masculine and feminine, with a gorgeous palate of **chocolate browns and clean bridal whites,** and plenty of soft candlelight and rustic wood accents.

invitations

Set the tone with rich chocolate brown invitations with white writing. Either go to a local stationery store and order heavy chocolate card stock engraved or thermographed in white, or pick up the card stock and write on it yourself with a white or silver pen. Invite your guests to "come meet the lovebirds" and enclose two feathers (find them at craft stores), one white and one brown, in a dark brown envelope. Address the envelopes in your nicest script with a white or silver pen.

decor

Start with a color scheme of chocolate brown and white, and add rustic, woodsy accent pieces.

- **Line a table with a white tablecloth** or runner, and then set twig or wooden place mats (found at most home stores or Asian markets) at each seat.
- **Roll white napkins** in wooden or faux tortoiseshell napkin rings (you can purchase an inexpensive version at most dollar stores). Stick a brown feather into each napkin ring, too.
- **Look for brown transferware** or brown toile dishes (these are antique-looking plates with intricate brown-on-white patterns—they're romantic and masculine at the same time) in different patterns. After the dinner, you could give the dishes to the couple as an engagement present or early wedding gift. Look for these at department stores and antique shops and flea markets. Don't be afraid to mix and match.
- **Collect branches from outside** to use in a centerpiece or to adorn the table.
- **Use clear water and wine glasses**— funky, playful water glasses with more elegant wine glasses—and place them to the upper right of the dinner plates.
- If you can find any **cutlery with twig-like handles,** mix that in with your other flatware.
- **Make Monogram Breadsticks** (page 129) in the shape of the initials of your guests and use these as place cards.
- **Place white tea lights** all around the table. For a more over-the-top touch, scatter white feathers on the table and inside miniature birdcages, which you can find at dollhouse or craft stores.
- **Call your local pet store** to see if you can rent a birdcage with two lovebirds. It's worth a try!

music

Try romantic jazz—check online or your local record store for compilations of various artists, such as the two-disc *Jazz for Romantic Moments.*

party favors

Give guests a romantic little goody to take home, such as miniature birdcages filled with little chocolates wrapped in fall-colored foil, available in season at drugstores and candy stores. For the guests of honor, if not giving them dishes, consider stationery engraved with their new initials.

menu

Start with a champagne toast, then enjoy red wine and a romantic menu of autumn-inspired foods.

champagne

red wine

monogram breadsticks

stacked spinach and wild rice salad

grilled lamb chops with walnut pesto and apricot chutney

broiled portobello mushrooms

chamomile tea

rustic apple and pear tarts with fresh figs

monogram breadsticks

MAKES 16 BREADSTICKS

These are great for a party. They are shaped and styled by you and baked in your home, so no one has to know they came from a can! These breadsticks make great edible place cards. Make initials for each of your guests, and put them on plates on the table so guests can find their places before being seated.

Two 11-ounce cans refrigerated soft breadsticks
3 tablespoons butter, melted
Minced tea leaves, chopped fresh rosemary, chopped fresh chives, sea salt, grated Parmesan cheese, chopped dried lavender, garlic or onion powder, or sesame seeds for sprinkling on top

Preheat the oven to 350°F. Line a baking sheet with parchment paper or aluminum foil.

Separate the dough and shape into 8 long breadsticks per can for 16 breadsticks total. Brush with butter and sprinkle with the toppings of your choice.

Twist and shape the dough into initials and place on the prepared baking sheet. Bake in batches for 14 to 18 minutes, or until golden brown. Remove from the oven and set aside to cool. Place the breadsticks at each table setting before your guests arrive.

stacked spinach and wild rice salad

SERVES 8

This is an amazing presentation for an easy salad that has bursts of flavor in each bite thanks to corn, feta cheese, dried cranberries, fresh pears, and walnuts. You can assemble the salads in advance if you'd like (see Tea Party Tip), and there is no cooking other than preparing wild rice according to the package directions. You'll need one empty six-ounce tuna can, washed and dried, with the top and bottom lids removed.

TEA PARTY TIP

To make the salads in advance, you'll need 8 tuna cans. Place them on a baking sheet and spray the sheet and the insides of the cans with nonstick cooking spray. Assemble the individual portions in the cans and leave the cans on the sheet. Cover with plastic wrap and refrigerate for up to 8 hours. To plate and serve, line up 8 salad plates near the baking sheet. Use a spatula to lift a can onto each plate. Gently remove the cans.

One-half 6-ounce box instant wild rice
One 8-ounce bottle balsamic vinaigrette dressing
One 6-ounce package prewashed fresh baby spinach
One 11-ounce can corn niblets, drained
2 cups (8 ounces) crumbled feta cheese
2 cups dried cranberries
2 pears, cored and thinly sliced
½ cup chopped walnuts

Prepare the wild rice according to the package directions. Set aside to cool completely.

Set the empty tuna can on a salad plate and spoon a 1-inch layer of wild rice into the can. Drizzle with a little dressing, then top with a thin layer of spinach leaves and drizzle with a little more dressing. Add a thin layer of corn, a thin layer of feta, a thin layer of cranberries, and then a thin layer of pear slices, and drizzle with more dressing. Sprinkle some walnuts on top. Pressing down gently with one hand, remove the tuna can with the other. Repeat the process to make 7 more servings. Drizzle a little dressing around the plates before serving, if desired.

grilled lamb chops with walnut pesto and apricot chutney

SERVES 8

The sweet of the chutney plays against the earthy pesto in this elegant main course that's perfect for a rustic dinner party. Although it sounds difficult, it couldn't be easier: Buy the chutney and the pesto at a gourmet store or online.

One 8-ounce container walnut pesto
16 individual baby lamb chops
6 tablespoons chopped black tea leaves
One 6-ounce jar apricot chutney
Broiled Portobello Mushrooms (page 132)

Heat your grill to medium or a grill pan over medium heat.

Pour the pesto into a large, shallow dish. Place the lamb chops in the dish and turn to coat each side with pesto. Put the tea on a medium plate. Dip each side of the pesto-coated chops into the tea. Grill the lamb chops for 6 to 9 minutes, turning once, for medium rare.

Serve the lamb chops family style on a large platter, arranging them around a bowl filled with the chutney. Have the ends of the lamb chops face out so they are easy to pick up as they are passed. Serve the portobello mushrooms on the side.

broiled portobello mushrooms

SERVES 8

Portobellos have a mild yet deep flavor that is complemented by a sprinkling of tea leaves before broiling. This wonderfully simple recipe uses just a few ingredients to showcase these beautiful mushrooms.

8 large portobello mushroom caps
2 tablespoons olive oil
1 tablespoon chopped Ceylon tea leaves
Salt and pepper

Preheat the broiler. Line a shallow pan with aluminum foil.

Clean the mushrooms with a damp towel. Place the mushrooms, rounded side up, in one layer in the pan and lightly brush them with the olive oil. Sprinkle with the tea leaves and salt and pepper. Broil for 5 to 7 minutes, or until tender. Serve hot.

rustic apple and pear tarts with fresh figs

SERVES 8

I am almost embarrassed to call this a recipe—it's so easy. I always store puff pastry
sheets in my freezer so I can create a beautiful dessert in no time, anytime. These tarts
are a treat when fresh figs are in season in the early fall, and are delicious served with
a scoop of vanilla ice cream. You could leave out the preserves and figs and bake
these tarts a day or two in advance. Reheat them in a 275-degree oven for ten minutes before glazing and adding the figs.

One 17.5-ounce package frozen puff pastry
Sugar, for sprinkling
2 apples, halved, cored, and thinly sliced
2 pears, halved, cored, and thinly sliced
1 cup apricot preserves, warmed
8 fresh figs, thinly sliced

Thaw the pastry at room temperature for 20 minutes.

Preheat the oven to 400°F. Line a baking sheet with parchment paper.

Unfold 2 pastry sheets on a lightly floured surface. Using a rotary pastry
cutter or a knife, make 8 strips from each sheet.

Sprinkle the pastry with sugar and lay 4 to 6 slices of apple or pear on each
strip of pastry, arranging the fruit on an angle, and overlapping the slices.
Sprinkle each tart with a little more sugar. You should have 8 apple tarts and
8 pear tarts.

Arrange the tarts on the prepared baking sheet, and bake for 20 minutes,
or until golden brown.

Remove the tarts from the oven and brush the warm preserves on top with
a pastry brush. Top the tarts with the figs. Serve 1 pear and 1 apple tart per
person, warm or at room temperature.

Iceberg Blue
A44-4

Daddy's Little Girl
A7-3

I
A445

Given with love by Katie and Christie
September 16 at 1 p.m.
90 Commonwealth Avenue, Boston

Pleased as Punch
A7-4

Given with love by Katie and Christie
September 16 at 1 p.m.
90 Commonwealth Avenue, Boston

Cherry Grove
A7-5

BABY SHOWER
luncheon

Celebrate a friend's good news with a fun luncheon. If you know whether she's having a boy or a girl, create the party around the **appropriate blue or pink color** scheme. If you don't know, go with a perfectly appropriate pale yellow theme. No matter what the color scheme, serve plenty of delicious food the mommy-to-be will love.

invitations

Get paint color strips in the appropriate color—something that might inspire the paint color in a nursery—from a local paint shop or hardware store. Print the invitation information on a sticker that will fit on the strip along with "It's a Boy!," "It's a Girl!," or "It's a Baby!"

decor

Work the color scheme throughout the luncheon. Make this festive and pretty, just right for an expectant mom.

- **Cover tables** in pale blue, pink, or yellow cloths, and use coordinating napkins.
- **Get flowers** in the same color and have bunches of them around the room.
- **Buy M&Ms in just one color** (pale pink, pale blue, or pale yellow) and place them in glass containers around the table and the room.
- **Use white plates,** and make place mats out of paper decorated with rubber stamps of little baby carriages, bottles, pacifiers, and other baby-themed images—in ink to match the color scheme. (You can find rubber stamps and ink pads at paper stores and online.)

music

Prepare a mix of "baby" music, including songs such as "Be My Baby" and "Baby, I Love You."

party favors

Fill baby bottles with the single-color M&Ms and tie the bottles with coordinating ribbon. Make extra sheets of decorated paper, punch holes in one corner of each sheet, and tie the sheets together with ribbon to make a "Baby's First Scrapbook" for the guest of honor.

To save time, make cupcakes from your favorite vanilla cake mix. Buy your favorite vanilla frosting and tint it pale blue, pink, or yellow. To make the cupcakes look really pretty, pipe the frosting onto the cupcakes in a swirl using a pastry bag fitted with a round or star tip.

menu

This is hearty enough to satisfy someone who's eating for two, but light enough to please the rest of your guests.

decaffeinated vanilla black tea

sparkling white grape juice

prosecco or other sparkling wine

mini chicken and arugula sandwiches

tomato basil salad with mini mozzarella

corkscrew pasta with chickpeas, roasted red peppers,
and parmesan

vanilla cupcakes with tinted frosting
(to match the color scheme; see page 62)

mini chicken and arugula sandwiches

MAKES 10 TEA SANDWICHES

These small sandwiches have a tasty little bite from the red onion and arugula that works well with the somewhat salty olive bread. If you need to, you can prepare the chicken a few hours or a day in advance and, once it cools, keep it refrigerated with the skillet sauce until you're ready to assemble the sandwiches. But keep in mind that these sandwiches are very tasty when the chicken is still warm.

6 tablespoons olive oil
1 pound chicken cutlets, thinly pounded
Salt and pepper
1½ tablespoons chopped fresh thyme
2 garlic cloves, finely chopped
3 tablespoons balsamic vinegar
10 slices olive bread
½ medium red onion, thinly sliced
1 bunch of arugula

Heat 2 tablespoons of the olive oil in a large skillet over medium-high heat. Sprinkle the chicken cutlets on both sides with salt, pepper, and 1 tablespoon of the thyme. Add the chicken to the pan in batches and sauté until golden and cooked through, about 2 minutes per side. Remove the chicken from the skillet.

Add the remaining 4 tablespoons of the oil and the garlic to the skillet. Stir over medium heat for about 15 seconds. Add the vinegar and the remaining ½ tablespoon of the thyme. Cook for 15 seconds, scraping up browned bits from the bottom of the pan. Return the chicken to the skillet and toss until it's heated through, about 1 minute.

Halve each slice of bread and then lay half the bread slices out on a serving platter. Divide the chicken, onion, and arugula among the bread slices on the platter, then drizzle each sandwich with a bit of the skillet sauce. Top with the remaining bread slices.

tomato basil salad with mini mozzarella

Everyone loves this classic salad. It's healthy and substantial at the same time. Make this ahead of time and refrigerate it for up to a day.

5 pounds ripe tomatoes, cut into wedges
¾ cup extra-virgin olive oil
1½ cups torn fresh basil leaves
2 cups (8 ounces) mini mozzarella balls
Salt and pepper

Toss the tomatoes with the olive oil in a serving dish. Add the basil and mozzarella and toss again. Season with salt and pepper to taste.

corkscrew pasta with chickpeas, roasted red peppers, and parmesan

SERVES 10

Forget low-carb! This salad, punctuated with beans, roasted red peppers, and cheese, is especially tasty if you assemble it at least an hour or two in advance to give the flavors time to come together. If you make it the day before, keep it covered in the refrigerator, and take it out an hour or so before you serve it so it comes to room temperature.

1¼ boxes (1¼ pounds) corkscrew pasta
⅓ cup chopped fresh mint, plus more for garnish
1 tablespoon grated lemon zest
3 tablespoons lemon juice
3 tablespoons dry white wine
2 garlic cloves, chopped
6 tablespoons olive oil
Two 7-ounce jars roasted red peppers, drained and cut into strips
One 15- or 16-ounce can chickpeas, drained
½ cup grated Parmesan cheese
Salt and black pepper

Bring a large pot of salted water to a boil over high heat. Add the pasta and cook according to the package directions, until tender but still a little firm. Drain it, rinse with cold water to cool, and then drain again.

Combine the mint, lemon zest, lemon juice, wine, and garlic in a large bowl. Whisk in the oil. Add the pasta, roasted red peppers, chickpeas, and cheese. Toss everything together. Season the mixture with salt and pepper to taste and toss again. Before serving, garnish with extra chopped mint.

CHILDREN'S
tea party

This party is all about fun and introducing children to the wonderful custom of drinking tea. It's absolutely delightful for a **little girl's birthday party** lunch or an afternoon tea where dolls are the primary guests. It should be colorful (**multicolored polka dots** are an easy motif to use), pretty, and sweet—a child's fantasy tea.

invitations

Create a CD of the favorite music of the child "hosting" the party. Print pink and orange polka dots on the background of CD stickers, and write the invitation information on the sticker with a vivid pink pen.

decor

Go with bright colors such as pink and orange, polka dots, and glitter, and any other fun, girly accents you can think of.

- **Have everything set up** for a Hula-Hoop contest when all the guests arrive. Have a Hula-Hoop for each child—get them in bright pink and orange—and let them practice for a few minutes. Whoever goes the longest might win the honor of pouring the tea.
- **Line the table** with a bright orange cloth.
- **Write the guests' names** on bright pink and orange place cards with glitter glue. Drape little pink boas or fairy wings (you can find them at toy stores or online) over the back of each chair. The girls can wrap themselves in the boas as they're settling in for tea.
- **You might have a tiara** for the guest of honor to wear, or one for everyone.
- **Serve the tea sandwiches,** scones, and pastries on traditional tiered trays, and teach the girls that at tea, you start from the bottom tier with tea sandwiches and work your way up to the sweets on top.

music

Play the CD of favorite music that you sent with the invitation, and have similar music choices ready to go.

party favors

Bake sugar cookies in the shape of teapots before the party and bring out tubes of decorating icing and sprinkles. Let the guests decorate their own teapot-shaped cookie to take home. Have them decorate the cookies right after the Hula-Hoop contest and then set them aside to dry. At the end of the party, place them in clear cellophane bags tied with bright pink and orange ribbons.

TEA PARTY TIP

For mini cupcakes, make the cupcake batter from page 62 or from your favorite cake mix, and bake tiny cupcakes in a mini-muffin pan for 15 to 18 minutes. Divide your frosting into two halves and color half of the cooled cupcakes with bright pink food coloring and the other half with bright orange food coloring. Top the frosting with a few polka dot sprinkles.

menu

Everything from the tea to the sandwiches to the dessert on this menu is great for kids. They'll have a hard time going back to their standard mealtime fare!

rooibos tea or other herbal tea

TEA SANDWICHES

peanut butter and banana

raisin bread and apple butter

strawberry cream cheese

strawberry scones and clotted cream (page 39)

mini cupcakes (page 144)

vanilla tea–infused sugar cookies

peanut butter and banana tea sandwiches

MAKES 6 TEA SANDWICHES

This classic combination was one of Elvis's favorites. (Add one or two of his songs to the party playlist!) Make these easy sandwiches fairly close to serving time so the bread doesn't get soggy. If you'll need to make them an hour or more in advance, spread the bread with a very thin layer of butter before assembling the sandwiches.

12 thin slices white bread
⅓ cup creamy peanut butter
2 very ripe bananas, mashed

Using a large flower-shaped cookie cutter (about 2½ inches across), cut a flower out of each slice of bread. Spread 6 of the flowers with a layer of peanut butter and then add a thin layer of mashed banana. Top with the remaining flowers and press gently to close. Serve immediately or refrigerate, wrapped in plastic, until ready to serve or for up to 3 hours.

raisin bread and apple butter tea sandwiches

This is another easy and appealing sandwich, made with sweet bread and store-bought apple butter.

6 thin slices raisin bread, crusts trimmed
¼ cup store-bought apple butter

Spread a thin layer of apple butter on 3 of the slices of bread. Top with the remaining slices of bread and press gently. Cut each on the diagonal into 2 triangles to make 6 sandwiches. Serve immediately or refrigerate, wrapped in plastic, until ready to serve or for up to 3 hours.

strawberry cream cheese tea sandwiches

MAKES 6 TEA SANDWICHES

This is a simple sandwich to make, but it is one of my daughter's favorites. If you'd like to make your own strawberry cream cheese, puree one-quarter cup chopped fresh strawberries and then blend them with three ounces softened regular cream cheese.

12 thin slices whole wheat bread
½ cup (4 ounces) strawberry cream cheese

Using a large heart-shaped cookie cutter (about 2½ inches across), cut a heart out of each slice of bread. Spread a layer of cream cheese on 6 of the hearts then top the cream cheese with the remaining hearts. Press gently to close the sandwiches. Serve immediately or refrigerate, wrapped in plastic, until ready to serve or for up to 3 hours.

strawberry scones

MAKES 8 SCONES

These delicious sweet and fruity scones are great for any afternoon tea, but especially appropriate for children's tea. You'll need to refrigerate this dough for at least an hour (or overnight) before slicing it, adding the strawberries, and baking it.

1¾ cups all-purpose flour, or more if needed

2 teaspoons baking powder

½ stick (4 tablespoons) unsalted butter, chilled

¼ cup plus 1 tablespoon milk

½ cup orange juice concentrate (defrosted if frozen)

2 teaspoons grated lemon zest

1½ pints fresh strawberries, hulled and sliced

¼ cup strawberry jam

1 large egg

Whisk together the flour and baking powder in a large bowl. Cut in the cold butter with a fork or pastry blender until the mixture resembles coarse crumbs. Make a well in the center of the mixture, pour in the milk, and mix together with a rubber spatula until the dough forms a sticky ball. Mix the orange juice concentrate and lemon zest together and add to the dough. Work in a tablespoon or two of extra flour if the dough is too sticky to work with. On a lightly floured surface, pat the dough into a 1-inch-thick circle, then wrap it in plastic, and refrigerate it for at least 1 hour.

Preheat the oven to 400°F. and prepare a baking sheet by sprinkling it with flour.

Using a serrated knife, cut the dough into 2 layers horizontally. Place the bottom half of the dough on the prepared baking sheet. Distribute the strawberries and dollops of jam evenly over the dough layer. Lay the top layer of dough over the strawberry layer and pinch the edges together to seal.

Cut the dough into 8 wedges. Lightly beat the egg in a small dish and brush it over the wedges. Bake until the scones are golden on top and a tester or toothpick inserted into the center of a scone comes out clean, about 14 minutes. Cool the scones on the sheet for at least 5 minutes. Serve warm or at room temperature.

vanilla tea–infused sugar cookies

MAKES ABOUT 40 COOKIES

Of course, you can make your favorite sugar cookie dough recipe instead (maybe it's infused with a hint of citrus or almond extract or just plain vanilla), or you can make these—they're slightly crisp on the outside and soft inside—and let your young guests know that tea is a special ingredient. Keep in mind: You need to make the dough at least four hours before you bake these cookies so you have time to chill it before you roll it out to cut it.

2 sticks (1 cup) unsalted butter, softened
⅔ cup sugar
1 large egg
1 teaspoon vanilla extract
2½ cups all-purpose flour
1 teaspoon ground decaffeinated vanilla black tea leaves
½ teaspoon salt

With an electric mixer, beat together the butter and sugar until smooth and fluffy. Beat in the egg. Add the vanilla.

In a separate bowl, whisk together the flour, tea leaves, and salt. Add the dry ingredients to the butter mixture and mix until just combined. Wrap the dough in plastic and chill for at least 4 hours or overnight.

Preheat the oven to 350°F.

On a lightly floured surface, roll out the dough to about ¼ inch thick. Using a teapot-shaped cookie cutter (or another favorite shape), cut out the cookies and transfer them to an ungreased baking sheet. Bake for 8 to 10 minutes, until just turning golden. Remove from the oven and cool on a wire rack.

Serve the cookies warm with tea, or let them cool completely before frosting and decorating them.

SUMMER
picnic
FOR 8

Take the idea of an old-fashioned afternoon picnic and mix things up with an **Asian theme** and the Asian flavors that taste so fresh and good on a summer day. Set up **Japanese umbrellas** and straw mats instead of the traditional plaid blankets. Serve your drinks with vibrant little umbrellas, present food in bento boxes, and string Japanese lanterns from nearby trees.

invitations

Purchase inexpensive Asian-inspired folding fans from a gift shop or online and attach a note that says, "You're invited to keep cool at a refreshing summer picnic." Mail the fan and invitation in a large, bright, summery-colored envelope.

decor

Being outside creates a lush and summery backdrop, which you can enhance with Asian-inspired touches.

- **Go to an Asian supermarket** or home goods store to find large paper umbrellas and straw mats to place on the ground instead of blankets (both the umbrellas and mats are lightweight and inexpensive).
- **Present your picnic food** in picnic-style bento boxes (boxes divided into compartments) prepared in advance for each guest. You can get acrylic ones at many kitchen stores, or disposable ones from Asian groceries or from a local Japanese restaurant. Wrap sandwiches in wax paper (twisted at the ends) and place them in the bento boxes along with Asian slaw in a small takeout container and fruit salad. Pack in a cooler with ice packs.
- **Keep iced tea and lemonade cold** in thermoses or small coolers.
- Instead of standard utensils, **pack disposable chopsticks.** Buy colorful paper napkins, drink umbrellas, and brightly colored plastic cups and tote everything in a wicker basket (for a touch of that traditional picnic feel).

party favors

Send guests home with Chinese takeout containers, which you can get from your local Chinese takeout place, filled with fortune cookies.

music

Bring a portable CD player and play a compilation of Japanese music or the soundtrack from *Lost in Translation.*

menu

A picnic becomes more exotic with this Asian-inspired fare.

iced tea with sliced fresh ginger

lemonade with mint

sake and ginger tea cocktails

thai chicken wraps

vegetarian sushi rolls

asian slaw with peanuts

gingered fruit salad

sake and ginger tea cocktails

SERVES 8

Brew the ginger tea ahead of time and chill it, and then prepare a thermos of this cocktail to bring with you on your picnic.

1 cup chilled sake
2 cups chilled vodka
1 cup chilled ginger tea
Ice
Candied ginger (in small pieces), for garnish

Combine the sake, vodka, and ginger tea in a large pitcher filled one-quarter full with ice. Mix well and strain into a thermos. Pour into plastic cups at your picnic, garnish with candied ginger, and serve.

TEA PARTY TIP

Vary this cocktail by using chilled lemon tea instead of ginger tea and slipping a lemon drop candy into the bottom of the cup when you serve it.

thai chicken wraps

MAKES 8 WRAPS

The peanut sauce for these wraps makes them really special, and it's easy to prepare. You can make it a day in advance and refrigerate it. To save time, you could use purchased Thai peanut sauce.

¼ cup creamy peanut butter
¼ cup sugar
3 tablespoons soy sauce
2 tablespoons vegetable oil
1 teaspoon minced garlic
1 pound precooked chicken breast strips
½ teaspoon salt
½ teaspoon pepper
Eight 8-inch soft-flour tortillas
4 cups shredded lettuce
1 medium red onion, thinly sliced
2 teaspoons grated fresh ginger

Make a peanut sauce by combining the peanut butter, sugar, soy sauce, vegetable oil, garlic, and 3 tablespoons water in a small saucepan over low heat. Heat until the sugar is dissolved, stirring frequently. Set aside to cool.

   In a medium bowl, toss the chicken with the salt and pepper. To assemble the wraps, spread each tortilla with some of the peanut sauce. Divide the chicken, lettuce, onion, and ginger evenly among the tortillas. Roll up the tortillas, folding the ends in as you go, and wrap them in wax paper or colored plastic wrap, twisting the ends to secure.

asian slaw with peanuts

SERVES 8

Skip the potato salad and traditional coleslaw in favor of this kicky and delicious salad that travels well. Make this an hour or two before it's time to leave for your picnic and let it sit in the fridge so the flavors have time to come together.

2 tablespoons rice wine vinegar

2 tablespoons soy sauce

5 tablespoons vegetable oil

2 tablespoons sesame oil

2 tablespoons grated fresh ginger

1 small head napa cabbage, thinly sliced

1 large carrot, peeled and cut into thin matchsticks

2 medium green bell peppers, seeded and cut into 2-inch-long strips

1 cup snow peas, stringed and thinly sliced lengthwise

3 scallions, sliced

¼ cup chopped fresh cilantro leaves

½ cup roasted peanuts

In a small bowl, whisk together the vinegar, soy sauce, vegetable and sesame oils, and ginger. Set aside.

In a large bowl, mix together the cabbage, carrot, peppers, snow peas, scallions, cilantro, and peanuts. Add the dressing and toss well.

gingered fruit salad

SERVES 8

Ginger adds zing to a summery fruit salad. Use any kind of berries you like here. You could replace some of the fruit with chunks of pineapple or mango, too.

½ **cup sugar**
½ **cup thinly sliced fresh ginger**
2 pints fresh mixed berries (blueberries, raspberries, and strawberries)
3 white peaches or nectarines, sliced
½ **small cantaloupe or honeydew melon, seeded, flesh cut into 1-inch chunks**
¼ **cup chopped fresh mint leaves**

Bring the sugar, ginger, and ¾ cup water to a boil in a medium saucepan. Stir until the sugar is dissolved. Simmer for 10 minutes, then remove from the heat and let sit for 20 minutes. Pour the syrup through a strainer into a bowl, discarding the ginger. Chill, covered, for 2 hours.

Combine the berries, peaches, and melon in a large bowl with the mint and ½ cup of the syrup and toss to coat. Serve immediately or cover and refrigerate for up to a day.

ARTIST
tea

Celebrate your favorite emerging artists with a dinner in their honor. In the last century, this is what tea salons were all about: patrons and sponsors of the arts bringing people together to admire, inspire, relax, and talk. This party should be filled with color, **creativity, artful flair,** and lots of food—don't let the starving artists go hungry!

invitations

Find art postcards at a local art museum, stationery store, or online, and write a simple invitation on the back.

decor

Vivid colors and plenty of artistic accents set the tone for this party.

- **Scatter framed museum art postcards** around the table and the room.
- **Use small watercolor sets** (available at art supply stores) painted with names as place cards.
- **For your centerpiece,** stack vibrant, colorful art books on the table. Or create a centerpiece that might inspire a still life, with bowls of fruit and a jug of wine.
- **Use paper for a tablecloth,** and set out painted coffee cans filled with crayons and colored pencils so guests can express their creativity.
- **Set the table with black** or dark wooden chargers, and serve food on glass plates in stacks of two with colorful art prints or postcards sandwiched between them.

music

Play selections of innovative jazz or twentieth-century American composers, such as John Cage.

party favors

Let guests keep the creativity flowing at home—give them drawing tablets and colored pencils or crayons and have them take home their watercolor sets.

menu

This is a filling and wonderful menu that a working artist will greatly appreciate—and so will all patrons of the arts. Ceylon tea is a strong black tea that goes well with the hearty flavors on this menu.

ceylon tea

red and white wine

ceylon cheese crisps

ceylon tea steak au poivre with garlic cream sauce

homemade potato fries with ceylon tea salt

frisée salad with sherry vinaigrette

ceylon tea-scented crème brûlée

(See recipe for Lavender Tea–Scented Crème Brûlée, page 82.
Replace the lavender tea with Ceylon tea.)

ceylon cheese crisps

MAKES ABOUT 24 CRISPS

These homemade treats, a cross between a cracker and a tuile, are easy, delicious, and great with a glass of wine to start off the night. Make them in advance because you need to refrigerate the dough for at least eight hours before baking. Serve them with an assortment of fresh fruit, such as raspberries, blueberries, grapes, and apple slices.

2 sticks (1 cup) unsalted butter, softened
1¼ cups all-purpose flour
¼ teaspoon cayenne pepper
2 cups (8 ounces) grated Cheddar cheese
1 teaspoon chopped Ceylon tea leaves
1 teaspoon salt

Combine the butter, flour, cayenne, cheese, and tea leaves in a medium bowl, mixing thoroughly. On a lightly floured surface, form two logs, each about 1½ inches in diameter. Wrap the logs in wax paper and then foil and refrigerate for at least 8 hours, or overnight.

Preheat the oven to 375°F. and line 2 baking sheets with parchment paper.

Working with one log at a time, slice the dough into thin wafers (about 12 per log) and bake on the prepared sheets for 6 to 10 minutes (depending on the thickness of the wafers) until they are light golden and just firm to the touch. Watch closely—you don't want them to burn! Let the crisps cool on the sheets for 2 minutes and then transfer them to wire racks to cool. Before serving, flip the crisps over and sprinkle them with the salt.

ceylon tea steak au poivre
with garlic cream sauce

SERVES 8

This recipe will inspire and satisfy all your guests. Each steak is enough to serve two people.

2 tablespoons unsalted butter

4 large garlic cloves, chopped

2 cups heavy cream

2 tablespoons plus 1 teaspoon Ceylon tea leaves

1 beef bouillon cube

Salt and pepper

Four 1-pound boneless sirloin steaks, about 1 inch thick

2 tablespoons coarsely ground black pepper

To make the sauce, melt the butter in a medium saucepan over medium-low heat. Add the garlic and sauté for about 5 minutes. Add the heavy cream and 1 teaspoon of the tea leaves and bring to a simmer. Stir in the bouillon cube and season with salt and pepper. Simmer for another 10 minutes, until reduced and thickened. Cover and keep warm while you cook the steaks.

Heat a large nonstick grill pan over medium-high heat. Sprinkle the steaks on both sides with the coarse pepper and the remaining 2 tablespoons of the tea.

Grill the steaks for 4 to 5 minutes on each side for medium rare. Slice the steaks in half, pour the garlic cream sauce on top of the steaks, and serve immediately.

homemade potato fries with ceylon tea salt

SERVES 8

Potatoes are a food staple for starving artists. This recipe gives a new twist to an old standard.

5 pounds Idaho potatoes (about 5 large potatoes)
⅓ cup extra-virgin olive oil
2 tablespoons chopped Ceylon tea
1 teaspoon salt, plus more for serving
½ teaspoon black pepper

Scrub the potatoes well under cold running water; do not peel. Cut them into fingers about 3 inches long by ½-inch square. Place the potatoes in a large pot and cover them with cold water. Bring the water to a boil and cook for about 15 minutes, until the potatoes are nearly tender. Drain well.

Preheat the oven to 250°F.

Heat the oil in a large sauté pan over high heat. Season with the tea, salt, and pepper. Working in batches, add the potatoes and cook, tossing gently as needed, until they are browned and crispy, about 8 minutes. Use a slotted spoon to transfer the first batch of potatoes to a serving platter and place in the oven to keep warm while you finish the rest of the potatoes. Serve hot, sprinkled with additional salt if desired.

frisée salad with sherry vinaigrette

SERVES 8

This simple salad of beautiful frisée greens, toasted pecans, and creamy fresh goat cheese is topped with an easy homemade vinaigrette, which you can make in advance and store in the refrigerator for up to a week.

5 tablespoons sherry vinegar
1 medium shallot, finely chopped
1 tablespoon mustard seeds
1 tablespoon dry mustard
1 tablespoon honey
½ cup olive oil
Salt and pepper
1½ pounds frisée, leaves separated
¾ cup chopped toasted pecans
¾ cup crumbled fresh goat cheese

To make the vinaigrette, in a salad bowl whisk together the vinegar, shallot, mustard seeds, dry mustard, honey, and 1 tablespoon water. Whisk in the oil in a fine stream. Season the dressing with salt and pepper to taste.

Toss the frisée and pecans with the dressing, then sprinkle the goat cheese on top, and toss once or twice more before serving.

PALM BEACH
tea
FOR 8

This tea for ladies who lunch (or who want to pretend for a day to be ladies who lunch) is warm and welcoming with a festive Palm Beach theme. It's tea with a Florida twist. Use lots of crisp **kelly green and white** with **hints of coral** to set the mood.

invitations

Look for a preppy stationery motif, such as a bright green frog, and use coordinating stationery to create the invitations and place cards. Invite guests to a "Palm Beach luncheon" and encourage them to wear their favorite country club attire or Lilly Pulitzer dress, even in winter, when such a sunny tea would be especially welcome.

decor

Think chic and beachy—with bright green and white and coral accents and a few shells and starfish scattered about.

- **Skip the tablecloth.** Find palm fronds at a local florist or grocery store and layer them on your table interspersed with seashells, starfish, and coral branches—whatever you've scavenged from past trips to the beach.

- **Use white, wicker, or bamboo** place mats and coral napkins.

- **Try to use a mix** of coral, green, and white dishes—if you can find white dishes with a bright, modern coral pattern on them, that's perfect.

- **Keep the frog (or whatever you've chosen) motif going** with the place cards—if possible, use card stock that matches the invitation stock and write guests' names on them in pink or coral ink.

music

Play amusing and lighthearted tunes from the 1970s. Your guests will get a kick out of Tom Jones.

party favors

Give each guest a fun, pretty little etiquette book or beach-themed stationery (embossed with shells, starfish, or flip-flops) to take home.

menu

This is a quintessential menu for a luncheon for the ladies.

vanilla black tea

mimosas and bellinis

TEA SANDWICHES

cucumber and carrot

cream cheese and beet

egg salad (page 70)

scones (page 38) **with orange marmalade**
(or another citrus or tropical jelly)

mini lemon tarts

mimosa

MAKES 1 COCKTAIL

¼ **cup orange juice**
½ **cup (4 ounces) chilled champagne**

Pour the orange juice into a champagne flute. Add the champagne and serve.

bellini

MAKES 1 COCKTAIL

1 tablespoon pureed peach
Pinch of sugar (optional)
¾ **cup (6 ounces) chilled champagne**

Pour the peach puree into a champagne flute. Add a pinch of sugar if desired. Add the champagne and serve.

TEA PARTY TIP

Champagne is wonderful to mix with fresh fruit— the flavors complement each other perfectly. After you've tried the Mimosa and the Bellini, get creative with pureed strawberries and raspberries and other fruit juices.

cucumber and carrot tea sandwiches

MAKES 12 TEA SANDWICHES

Here's another twist on the classic cucumber tea sandwich, with a dash of orange color that makes it perfect for a Palm Beach party.

1 large cucumber, peeled and thinly sliced
Salt and white pepper
1 large carrot
12 thin slices white bread, crusts trimmed
1 stick (½ cup) unsalted butter, softened

Sprinkle the cucumber slices with salt and pepper and set aside in a colander so any excess liquid can drain out. Pat dry with paper towels. Peel the carrot, cut it into thirds, and thinly slice lengthwise with a mandoline or a sharp knife.

Cut each slice of bread in half. Coat each rectangle on one side with a very thin layer of butter. Line 2 to 3 cucumber slices on top of the buttered side of 12 of the rectangles. Add a tiny dab of butter and top with a carrot slice. Place another rectangle of bread on top, butter side down, and press the sandwiches together gently. Serve immediately or refrigerate, wrapped in plastic, until ready to serve or for up to 3 hours.

cream cheese and beet tea sandwiches

Cutting the bread into heart shapes and topping them with a vibrant beet slice makes these simple open-faced tea sandwiches look pretty and appealing. The beets add sweetness and a bit of texture that works well with the cream cheese.

12 thin slices wheat bread, toasted
¾ cup (6 ounces) cream cheese
12 canned beet slices
½ Granny Smith apple, peeled, cored, and grated
1 teaspoon lemon juice

Use a large heart-shaped cookie cutter (about 2½ inches across) to cut heart shapes out of each slice of wheat toast. Spread each piece of toast with the cream cheese, and then top with the beets. Toss the grated apple with the lemon juice, and garnish each beet with a pinch of grated apple. Serve immediately.

mini lemon tarts

MAKES 16 MINI TARTS

These are easy as pie—they feature store-bought pie crust and lemon curd, but you still get the wonderful aroma of a baking pie crust in your kitchen. Don't store these in the refrigerator. Keep them at room temperature for up to one hour once assembled.

One 15-ounce box refrigerated pie crust
One 12-ounce jar lemon curd
2 to 3 kiwis, thinly sliced

Preheat the oven to 400°F.

Using a cookie cutter or a drinking glass, cut sixteen 2-inch circles from the dough and press them into the slots of a mini-muffin pan. Prick the dough with the tines of a fork. Bake for about 15 minutes, or until golden brown, watching to make sure the edges don't burn. Remove from the oven, let the crusts cool in the pan for 15 minutes, unmold, and then let the crusts cool completely on a wire rack.

Scoop some lemon curd into each baked crust. Garnish each mini tart with a kiwi slice and serve.

TEA PARTY TIPS

Instead of kiwi, garnish the mini lemon tarts with fresh raspberries, mandarin orange sections, fresh blueberries, or fresh black-berries— be creative and you'll have several beautiful variations on this simple dessert.

Make mini cherry tarts from purchased pie crust and cherry pie filling. Follow the instructions on the packages to prepare—just be sure to cut narrow strips of pie crust dough to make a homemade-looking cross-hatch on top of the tarts.

FALL HARVEST
dinner
FOR 6 TO 8

This **cozy dinner** celebrates the season and features warm, comforting foods. Start collecting baby pumpkins, pinecones, and leaves in early fall so you'll have plenty to create an **autumnal atmosphere**.

invitations

Trace the shape of a large leaf onto heavy chocolate brown or orange paper and cut it out. Write the invitation on the leaf cutout in gold pen, and mail it in an oversized chocolate brown envelope.

decor

Rich chocolate brown, autumnal rusts and oranges, and hints of gold are perfect shades for this party, and they go well with the rustic natural accents of this time of year.

- **Serve dinner on an old dark wooden table.** Leave the wood exposed—use placemats or runners in fall harvest patterns if you want to add some color.
- **Scatter pinecones** and leaves around the table.
- **Cut open and clean out a few medium to large pumpkins,** and place vases inside filled with flowers, such as mums, and twigs. Do the same with miniature pumpkins, but fill the cavities with votive candles.
- **Set the table with orange dishes,** gold chargers, and wooden bowls to be filled with warm fall foods.
- **Look for napkins with a fall harvest print** with tones of brown and orange in the pattern, and roll them in dark brown tortoiseshell or wood napkin rings.

- **Make place cards from leaves**—write on them in chocolate brown ink.

music

Try the soundtracks from *When Harry Met Sally . . .* and *Autumn in New York.*

party favors

Fill brown paper bags with all the dry ingredients for scones (or a scone mix). Tie closed with twine and attach a wooden spoon and the recipe card.

menu

This fall menu features seasonal foods that are warm and comforting. Start with a soup course and then move on to the risotto course. Have plenty of warm bread on hand to accompany the soup.

spiced mulled wine

roasted butternut squash soup

wild mushroom risotto

chai tea with milk and honey (page 100)

apple-cranberry crisp

spiced mulled wine

SERVES 8

This drink fills your home with a delicious aroma and puts guests in a warm and happy mood to start the night off right. Double the recipe if you think guests will want more than one mugful.

Two 750-milliliter bottles dry red wine
Dash of bitters
1 tablespoon whole cloves
4 cinnamon sticks
1 tablespoon grated lemon zest
2 tablespoons sugar
1 teaspoon ground allspice

Combine the wine, bitters, cloves, cinnamon, lemon zest, sugar, and allspice in a heavy stockpot and heat gently over low heat for at least 20 minutes. Never let the mixture come to a boil. Strain the wine into mugs and serve.

roasted butternut squash soup

SERVES 8

The recipe for this delicious autumn soup comes from Christie, my coauthor, who taught her boyfriend, Will, how to make it—which he now does without ever looking at the recipe. It's that simple. You can serve this right away or make it up to two days in advance. If you do that, let it cool completely and then refrigerate it in an airtight container. Reheat it in a large stockpot (you might need to thin it with a little chicken stock) before serving. Serve in rustic-looking wooden bowls.

2 pounds store-bought precut fresh butternut squash
2 tablespoons olive oil
Salt and pepper
3 tablespoons butter
1 large onion, diced
1 Granny Smith apple, peeled, cored, and cut into chunks
12 fresh sage leaves
About 6 cups chicken broth
Pumpkin seeds, for garnish (optional)

Preheat the oven to 400°F.

Toss the butternut squash with the olive oil in a roasting pan, season with salt and pepper and roast for 20 minutes until somewhat softened and slightly browned.

Meanwhile, heat the butter in a large stockpot over medium heat. Add the onion and sauté for 3 minutes. Add the apple and sauté for another 2 minutes. Tear 4 of the sage leaves into small pieces, add to the pot, and cook for another 2 minutes. Add the squash and stir for 1 minute. Add 5 cups of the chicken broth and bring to a simmer. Simmer, uncovered, for 20 minutes, until the squash is very tender.

Use a hand blender to puree the soup right in the pot, or let the soup cool slightly and puree it in batches in your blender. Return the pureed soup to the pot and thin it with the remaining cup of broth if necessary. Season with salt and pepper to taste. Serve it in soup bowls and garnish with pumpkin seeds, if using, and the remaining fresh sage leaves.

wild mushroom risotto

SERVES 8

The mix of mushrooms in this savory risotto lends fabulous, almost meaty flavor that tastes wonderful after the slightly sweet butternut squash soup.

10 cups chicken broth
1 ounce dried porcini mushrooms
½ stick (4 tablespoons) unsalted butter
2 tablespoons olive oil
3 medium yellow onions, finely chopped
12 ounces cremini mushrooms, chopped
12 ounces shiitake mushrooms, stemmed and chopped
4 large garlic cloves, minced
1 tablespoon minced fresh thyme
2 tablespoons minced fresh marjoram
3 cups Arborio rice
1 cup dry white wine
1 cup grated Parmesan cheese, plus extra for serving
Salt and white pepper

Bring the broth to a simmer in a large saucepan. Add the porcini and simmer for 2 minutes. Use a slotted spoon to remove the porcini; set aside to cool, and then chop into ½-inch pieces. Cover the broth and keep warm.

Melt the butter with the oil in a large stockpot over medium heat. Add the onions and sauté for about 12 minutes, until softened. Add the cremini and shiitake and sauté until tender, about 8 minutes. Add the chopped porcini, garlic, thyme, and marjoram and sauté for 5 minutes. Add the rice and stir for about 3 minutes.

Add the wine and cook until the liquid is absorbed, stirring often, about 4 minutes. Add 1 cup of the warm chicken broth and simmer until the liquid is absorbed, stirring often, about 8 minutes. Continue to cook the rice, adding broth in 1-cup increments and stirring frequently, until it's just tender and the mixture is creamy. This should take 30 to 35 minutes.

Stir in the cheese and season with salt and pepper to taste. Serve immediately, with a bowl of Parmesan cheese for sprinkling at the table.

apple-cranberry crisp

SERVES 8

Fruit crisps are so easy to make and everyone loves them. You can prepare the topping and filling a few hours ahead of time. Combine them and bake them closer to serving time—the aroma of a baking crisp is delicious, and when you serve this warm with vanilla ice cream, your guests will be thrilled.

7 large Granny Smith apples
5 large Fuji apples
Juice of 1 lemon
2 sticks (1 cup) unsalted butter, softened
$\frac{1}{3}$ cup sugar
$1\frac{1}{2}$ cups packed brown sugar
2 teaspoons ground cinnamon
$\frac{1}{4}$ teaspoon ground nutmeg
$\frac{1}{4}$ teaspoon ground allspice
$1\frac{1}{2}$ cups all-purpose flour
$\frac{3}{4}$ cup sliced almonds
$\frac{1}{2}$ cup dried cranberries
1 pint vanilla ice cream

Preheat the oven to 350°F.

Peel, core, and slice the apples. Toss them in a bowl with the lemon juice to prevent discoloration.

Beat together the butter, sugar, brown sugar, cinnamon, nutmeg, and all-spice. Add the flour in increments and combine until the mixture has a coarse, crumbly texture. Stir in the almonds and cranberries.

Spread out the apples in a 13 × 9-inch baking dish. Distribute the cranberry-almond mixture evenly on top. Bake for about 45 minutes, until the apples are tender. Let cool for at least 8 to 10 minutes, and then serve warm or at room temperature with vanilla ice cream.

RUSSIAN
tea
FOR 8

Dramatic, sumptuous, and elegant, this party is one your guests will remember. It's a perfect way to surprise and delight people at cocktail hour during the cold winter months. **Velvets, faux furs, tassels,** rich red tones, and gold accents create a lavish atmosphere. Delicious Russian foods—caviar, cherries, **beet salad**, smoked salmon, Russian cookies—are a refreshing change from typical party fare.

invitations

Start with red card stock, and add a layer of shimmery gold vellum that has the invite information on it in black ink. To dress it up, add a small gold tea charm, which you can find at craft stores or online.

decor

The background color for this party is red. Add gold accents and use your most elegant serving pieces.

- **Start with a rich red tablecloth,** and consider adding place mats in velvet, jacquard, or damask.
- This is a good time to pull out **plates with gold leaf** or gold accents, if you have them.
- **Wrap vases with gold ribbon** and fill with bunches of deep red roses.
- **Use red napkins** and tie them with gold rope tassels for napkin rings.
- If you can find **gold-colored candlesticks** or candelabras, place red tapers in them and let the light flicker.
- **Use velvet** or faux fur–trimmed coasters.
- **Rent a Russian samovar** and glass teacups from a catering service to serve tea.
- **Make place cards** from red card stock with gold ink or gold paper with black ink.

music

Play classical music by great Russian composers such as Tchaikovsky.

party favors

Sweet chocolate eggs, which you can tell your guests are much more practical than fancy Fabergé eggs, are an ideal parting gift.

Traditional Russian tea is sweetened with the juice of black cherries, so serve black cherries along with black tea to give your guests a similar flavor combination. Or serve black cherry–flavored black tea, which you can find in many supermarkets and tea shops, or online.

menu

This is a simple, light menu for a small cocktail party. Serve the beet salads on small, easy-to-carry plates (or buffet style).

cranberry vodka martinis

caviar

beet salad with goat cheese

smoked salmon with mustard-dill sauce

russian black bread

lepeshki (russian cookies)

black cherries

black tea

caviar

If you decide to serve caviar, your guests will feel very special. There are a number of more affordable domestic versions available today that have wonderful flavor. Always buy caviar from a reputable source so you know it's of the highest quality. Here are a few tips for presenting it with panache.

- Serve caviar with mother-of-pearl spoons and forks if you have them; otherwise use wood or glass. Silver or stainless steel tends to give it a metallic taste.
- Keep caviar refrigerated until you serve it.
- Keep the tin or jar of caviar on a bed of crushed ice when serving.
- Allow about 2 ounces of caviar per person.
- Serve caviar with toast points (toasted bread triangles) or blinis (tiny pancakes, available at many gourmet stores).
- You can also serve caviar with plain water crackers or boiled and cooled potato slices.
- Crème fraîche, sour cream, crumbled hard-boiled eggs, and chopped onion are traditional accompaniments for caviar.

cranberry vodka martini

MAKES 1 COCKTAIL

This cocktail combines a deep shade of red (cranberries) with vodka—the perfect combination for a Russian tea.

6 tablespoons (3 ounces) cranberry vodka
Dash of lime juice
½ teaspoon sugar
Ice
3 or 4 fresh cranberries

Combine the vodka, lime juice, and sugar with ice in a cocktail shaker. Shake and strain into a chilled martini glass. Drop the fresh cranberries into the glass and serve.

ice buckets

Create a beautiful ice bucket for a bottle of vodka (or whatever spirit you want to chill) by placing the bottle in an empty 32-ounce milk or juice carton with the top cut off. Fill the carton around the bottle with a combination of water, cranberries, and a few sprigs of ivy or other greenery. (For other occasions, try adding citrus fruit slices, fresh herbs, grapes, or anything else that matches your decor.) Freeze until totally solid, and then remove the carton. Place your eye-catching ice bucket on your bar table, on a white or silver plate. The vodka will stay crisp and cold for quite some time.

beet salad with goat cheese

SERVES 8

The color of this salad goes well with a traditional Russian meal, and beets are defi-nitely quintessential Russian fare. You can make the vinaigrette up to two days in advance (keep it refrigerated in an airtight container), but you should assemble the salad close to serving time.

5 large red beets (about 2⅔ pounds)
2 large shallots, minced
3 tablespoons lemon juice
¾ teaspoon salt
¼ teaspoon pepper
⅓ cup plstachio oil or olive oil
4 cups baby greens
8 ounces fresh goat cheese
3 tablespoons salted shelled pistachios (not dyed red), coarsely chopped

Center a rack in the oven and preheat the oven to 425°F.

Wrap the beets tightly in two layers of foil and roast them in the oven until tender, about 1 hour. Unwrap the beets and let cool.

Meanwhile, make a dressing by whisking together the shallots, lemon juice, salt, and pepper in a small bowl. Add the oil in a fine stream, whisking constantly.

When the beets are cool enough to handle, slip off the skins and discard them. Cut the beets into 1-inch chunks and toss with ¼ cup of the dressing. In a separate bowl, toss the greens with the remaining dressing.

Make a pile of ½ cup of baby greens on each plate, and divide the beets into neat mounds among the plates. Drop spoonfuls of goat cheese on top of the beets. Sprinkle with pistachios and serve.

smoked salmon with mustard-dill sauce

SERVES 8

This simple, flavorful dish features smoked salmon, a traditional Russian food, and the flavor of fresh dill. Serve this with sliced Russian black bread on the side. You can make the sauce up to two days in advance; cover and refrigerate it after it's prepared.

⅓ cup honey mustard
2 tablespoons Dijon mustard
1½ tablespoons sugar
2½ teaspoons white wine vinegar
⅓ cup olive oil
¼ cup chopped fresh dill
Salt and pepper
1½ pounds smoked salmon, sliced

Whisk together the honey mustard, Dijon mustard, sugar, and vinegar in a medium bowl. Whisk in the oil in a fine stream and then stir in the dill. Season the sauce with salt and pepper to taste, keeping in mind that smoked salmon is salty. Arrange the salmon on a platter with the sauce on the side.

lepeshki (russian cookies)

MAKES ABOUT 24 COOKIES

These traditional cookies are subtly sweet and light and delicious with tea anytime. You can make them up to two days ahead and store them at room temperature in an airtight container.

2 cups self-rising flour
½ cup sugar
Pinch of salt
2 large egg whites
1 large egg yolk
½ cup sour cream
1 teaspoon vanilla extract
1 teaspoon almond extract
1 tablespoon milk
½ cup sliced almonds

Preheat the oven to 400°F. Lightly grease a baking sheet.

Whisk together the flour, sugar, and salt in a medium bowl. Make a well in the center of the dry ingredients.

Reserve about 2 tablespoons of egg white in a small bowl. Whisk the remaining whites with the egg yolk, sour cream, vanilla and almond extracts, and milk in a small bowl. Pour the sour cream mixture into the well in the dry ingredients and mix to form a soft dough.

Roll out the dough on a lightly floured surface until it's about ½ inch thick. Cut rounds with a 3-inch cookie cutter. Using a spatula, transfer the circles to your prepared baking sheet. Lightly beat the reserved egg white, then brush the cookies with it and sprinkle with the sliced almonds.

Bake for 10 minutes, until light golden brown. Cool on a wire rack.

WINTER WHITE tea

FOR 10 TO 12

Almost everything at this evening party is white. It's a very **elegant,** somewhat dramatic theme—one that many celebrities use for their parties. It can make for a winter wonderland of a holiday cocktail party, and is beautiful anytime you want to celebrate the season. Encourage guests to **dress all in white!**

invitations

Find white card stock shaped like snowflakes, or cut your own (you remember how!) from heavy paper. Write with silver ink, and place the invitations in white envelopes filled with white confetti and addressed in silver ink.

decor

Use white or glass everywhere—with touches of silver here and there.

- **Use white tablecloths** or placemats and napkins.
- **Use white dishes,** or place snowflake doilies under glass plates.
- **Use white or glass teacups** and saucers, and white sugar cubes in glass or white bowls.
- **Line the table with many white bowls** filled with Styrofoam or florist's foam, and insert as many white carnations as you can into each to create a white dome.
- **Scatter fake snow** or coconut flakes on the table around the flowers—see if you can make them resemble snowdrifts.
- **Frost glasses** with a snowflake stencil and glass etching spray (available at craft stores).
- **Serve food on white glass cake stands.**
- **Serve the soup in small white** or glass demitasse cups.

music

Play a selection of winter music. If this is a holiday party, include such favorites as "Frosty the Snowman" and "Winter Wonderland."

party favors

Give guests balls of white yarn stuck with white or metal knitting needles and include a simple hat pattern and a note (on white card stock and tied to the needles with white ribbon) wishing them a "warm winter."

white chocolate–dipped biscotti

Make purchased biscotti more special by dipping them into melted white chocolate. For an added winter white touch, dip them into white granulated sugar before the chocolate cools completely.

menu

The pale foods on this menu are anything but bland—they're packed with flavor!

white tea

white tea martinis with coconut (page 120)

TEA SANDWICHES

cucumber-mint (page 40)

turkey with parsley-shallot mayonnaise

goat cheese and white asparagus

white bean soup shooters

white truffle rice–stuffed mushrooms

white meringues
(Use basic meringue recipe, page 52)

white chocolate–dipped biscotti

vanilla ice cream with warm marshmallow sauce
and coconut flakes

turkey with parsley-shallot mayonnaise tea sandwiches

MAKES 24 TEA SANDWICHES

The flavors of parsley and shallot come together in a creamy mayonnaise to elevate the flavor of a simple turkey sandwich.

½ cup mayonnaise
3 tablespoons chopped fresh parsley
3 tablespoons minced shallot
½ teaspoon grated lemon zest
Salt and white pepper
12 thin slices white bread, crusts trimmed
10 ounces thinly sliced turkey

Mix the mayonnaise, parsley, shallot, and lemon zest in a small bowl. Season with salt and pepper. Spread the mayonnaise mixture on one side of each bread slice. Divide the turkey among 6 bread slices. Top with the remaining 6 bread slices, mayonnaise side down, pressing gently. Cut each sandwich diagonally into quarters. Serve immediately or refrigerate, wrapped in plastic, until ready to serve or for up to 3 hours.

goat cheese and white asparagus tea sandwiches

MAKES 12 TEA SANDWICHES

The prosciutto in this sandwich isn't white, but it adds such nice flavor.

1 pound thin white asparagus
Salt
12 thin slices white bread
One 8-ounce log goat cheese, chilled, cut into 12 thin slices lengthwise
4 ounces thinly sliced prosciutto

Cut the asparagus stalks in half and trim if necessary so they are the same length as the bread. Arrange the asparagus in a skillet large enough to hold it in one layer. Add ½ inch of salted cold water and cook the asparagus, covered, over moderately high heat for about 5 minutes, or until just tender. Drain well in a colander and run under cold water to stop the cooking process.

Trim the crusts from the bread and cut each slice in half into 2 rectangles. Make 12 sandwiches by layering 1 bread rectangle, 1 slice of goat cheese, some asparagus, and a slice of prosciutto. Trim excess prosciutto and cheese and top with another bread rectangle. Press gently together. Serve immediately or refrigerate, wrapped in plastic, until ready to serve or for up to 3 hours.

white bean soup shooters

MAKES 12 TO 15 SHOOTERS

This is a deliciously warm and filling soup. The rosemary lends it a wintry fragrance. Serving it in shooters instead of large bowls makes this perfect for a cocktail party.

1 large sprig fresh rosemary
1 medium onion, chopped
2 tablespoons olive oil
2 garlic cloves, minced
Two 15-ounce cans white beans, drained
6 cups chicken broth
Salt and white pepper

Chop enough rosemary leaves to equal 1 tablespoon, and reserve it, along with the rest of the sprig.

In a large stockpot over medium heat, sauté the onion with the olive oil until the onion is translucent, 6 to 8 minutes. Reduce the heat to low, add the garlic, and cook for another 3 minutes. Add the beans, rosemary sprig, and chicken broth. Cover, bring to a boil over high heat, then reduce the heat and simmer until the beans are very soft, 20 to 30 minutes. Remove the rosemary sprig.

Let the soup cool for 10 minutes and then use a hand blender to puree the soup right in the pot, or puree it in your blender in batches. Return the pureed soup to the pot and season with salt and pepper to taste. Serve in white or glass demitasse cups. Garnish with the reserved chopped rosemary.

white truffle rice–stuffed mushrooms

MAKES 20 HORS D'OEUVRES

These treats are a sophisticated take on traditional stuffed mushrooms. And they work beautifully with a pale color palette. You can make the filling ahead and refrigerate it in an airtight container for up to one day. Stuff and bake these mushrooms just before serving.

20 medium white mushrooms
Salt and white pepper
2 tablespoons unsalted butter
1 medium onion, finely chopped
1½ cups cooked white rice
2 teaspoons white truffle oil

Preheat the oven to 400°F. Spray a large, shallow baking pan with cooking spray.

Pull the stems from the mushroom caps. Finely chop the stems and set aside. Season the mushroom caps with salt and pepper and place them, rounded side up, in the prepared baking pan. Bake until the mushrooms are tender and start to release their liquid, about 10 minutes; remove them from the oven.

Meanwhile, melt the butter in a skillet over medium-high heat for a minute or two, until the foam goes down. Add the chopped mushroom stems and sauté, stirring, until golden, about 5 minutes. Add the onion and salt and pepper to taste and sauté, stirring occasionally, until the onion is golden, about 5 more minutes. Stir the mushroom mixture into the cooked rice along with the truffle oil. Season with salt and pepper to taste.

Turn the mushroom caps over and spoon the rice filling into the mushroom caps, pressing gently (there may be some filling left over). Bake until the mushrooms are tender, about 20 minutes. Remove from the oven and let cool for 5 minutes, then arrange on a tray and serve hot.

acknowledgments

I thank my mom and dad for being so creative, stylish, and, most important, loving.

Thanks to my beautiful and elegant grandmother who loves drinking tea.

To my husband, who walked into my tearoom and asked me out. I love your presence in my life.

To my sweet angels, who love attending tea parties.

To my most special circle of friends, new and old. You will always be cherished by me. You know who you are!

Thank you to the people who made this book possible: Michael, Christie, Rica, Ben, and Jane.

Thank you to the tea community, business acquaintances, vendors, retailers, press, celebrities, and fans who love my tea and support my business.

Special thanks to the people on the inside who have helped me to grow my company: Cesar, Dana, Kwasi, Tara, Michelle, Maggy, Jim, Lori, Lauren, Danielle, Marcia, Cathy, Christiaan, Jimmy, Jacob, Marie, Susan, Stuart, Jeff K., Laurie, and Patrick (the fashionable dandy).

Tea is my favorite ritual to share with the special people in my life and I believe in spreading sunshine to everyone I meet. I will always live my life with love and passion and I thank all of you for being so kind to me.

Enjoy life. Drink tea. Celebrate often.

—T.S.

Thanks to:

Tracy Stern for having innovative and beautiful vision, and for creating the most amazing collection of teas.

Rica Allannic for taking such good care of this manuscript and knowing what it takes to make a book fabulous.

Michael Bourret for introducing me to Tracy, giving this project so much love, and being a very cool afternoon tea companion.

Seth Matheson, Mandi Rutledge, Kevin O'Brien, Peter Kapinos, Scott Vlasak, and Karen Turley for tasting many of the recipes in this book and giving honest and enthusiastic feedback.

And Will Adams, for getting me permanently hooked on tea with a perfect cup of Earl Grey after a chilly morning swim in Canada—and for being my favorite person to drink tea with, anyplace, anytime.

—C.M.

resources

Here's a list of online resources that I like to use when planning my parties. Many have retail locations, too—you can find out about those on the Web sites. Happy hunting!

floral designers

Belle Fleur
www.bellefleurny.com
Fashionable flower and event designers that ship nationwide

Iris Rosin
www.irisrosin.com
New York–based floral stylist (who ships nationwide) and wedding and event planner

L'Olivier
www.lolivier.com
Chic, French, incredibly creative designs

food

British Delights
www.britishdelights.com
English tea, foods, and candies

Dean & Deluca
www.deananddeluca.com
Gourmet treats from caviar and foie gras to prepared hors d'oeuvres and pastries, plus a selection of tea

Formaggio Kitchen
www.formaggiokitchen.com
Artisan cheeses, chocolates, honeys, oils, vinegars, prepared sweets, and Dammann Freres teas

Gourmet Boutique
www.gourmetboutique.net
Caviar, tea, chocolates, and other European delicacies

Indian Foods Co.
www.indianfoodsco.com
Indian spices, foods, and teas

Payard
www.payard.com
The best frozen pastries and gourmet nibbles

Reva Paul Decorated Sugars
www.redwagonpress.com
Hand-decorated sugar cubes

Sur La Table
www.surlatable.com
Specialty and prepared foods and a large assortment of teakettles

Williams-Sonoma
www.williams-sonoma.com
All sorts of prepared foods, ingredients, and teas, and top-notch kitchen gadgets, cookware, teapots and teakettles, and chef's tools

invitations

Kate's Paperie
www.katespaperie.com
Beautiful stationery, cards, invitations, rubber stamps, wax seals, gift wrap, and ribbons

Paper Source
www.paper-source.com
Card stock; paper and envelopes in all shapes, colors, and sizes; plus ribbon, pens, paper punches, rubber stamps, ink, and more

party supplies

Party City
www.partycity.com
A discount party superstore, online

Plum Party
www.plumparty.com
Chic, cool supplies, party favors, and gifts for parties for every occasion

ShinDigZ
www.shindigz.com
Everything from basics such as balloons and banners to decorations for dozens of different party themes

tabletop

Apartment 48
www.apartment48.com
Home accessories and serving
pieces, including Moroccan tea
glasses and unique teapots

Bombay Company
www.bombaycompany.com
Porcelain and silver teapots and
serving pieces and other proper tea
accessories

Crate and Barrel
www.crateandbarrel.com
A wide selection of basic dishes and
glassware

Fishs Eddy
www.fishseddy.com
Retro and vintage serving pieces

Gracious Style
www.graciousstyle.com
Fine table linens, with monogram-
ming available

Horchow
www.horchow.com
Elegant dinnerware, glassware, and
linens, as well as prepared gourmet
foods

Jonathan Adler
www.jonathanadler.com
Colorful, modern, zany serving
pieces and table linens

The Well Dressed Home
www.welldressedhome.com
Vases and simple decorative elements, with many unique and
affordable pieces

West Elm
www.westelm.com
Contemporary dinnerware and
serving pieces

tea

Dean & Deluca
www.deananddeluca.com
(see page 203)

Tracy Stern SALONTEA
www.tracystern.com
My entire line of SALONTEAS and
BEAUTTEAS, as well as tea brewing
and serving products

Williams-Sonoma
www.williams-sonoma.com
(see page 203)

unusual party accessories

Heart to Heart Gifts
www.butterflycraze.com
Beautiful and whimsical butterflies,
flowers, and ladybugs to decorate
your party

Michaels
www.michaels.com
Craft supplies to create just about
anything you can think of

Miniatures
www.miniatures.com
Dollhouse miniatures of just about
anything you could imagine

Pearl River
www.pearlriver.com
Asian-inspired accessories, including
fabrics, Japanese lanterns, teapots,
and pretty Chinese takeout boxes

Sea Shell City
www.seashellcity.com
All kinds of shells, starfish, and
coral—perfect for beach-themed
parties

index

Page references in *italic* refer to photographs of recipes.